WHY SHOULD BRITAIN TREMBLE?

A Submariner's Tale

Chas Cooke

PublishAmerica
Baltimore

First printing

At the specific preference of the author, PublishAmerica allowed this work to remain exactly as the author intended, verbatim, without editorial input.

ISBN: 1-4241-1591-4
PUBLISHED BY PUBLISHAMERICA, LLLP
www.publishamerica.com
Baltimore

Printed in the United States of America

WHY SHOULD BRITAIN TREMBLE?

A Submariner's Tale

Chas Cooke

FOREWORD
BY THE AUTHOR

Although this book could be called an autobiography, I have tried to keep to a minimum the references to myself. This book is meant to be about those men that crewed the submarines and ships in which I served. Much of their behaviour you may find bizarre, and some of it possibly repulsive, but that is the way of men who serve in submarines.

The hardships of being confined, often for weeks on end, in a steel tube, several hundred feet beneath the sea, takes its toll on even those of the strongest character and a release has to be found for the frustrations that build up during a submarine patrol. This is often by way of strange and sometimes unsocial behaviour which members of the general public find hard to comprehend.

Perhaps this book will go some way to helping people understand why we acted as we did. If, during my travels around the world, in various submarines, I have caused offence or disruption to anyone, then I would like to take this chance to apologise and, if you were one of those, now reading this book, perhaps you will think a little more kindly of me at the end.

I have to mention the hardships suffered by my wife and children during my time at sea. They were often without a husband/father for many months and were required to be entirely self sufficient. It is a tribute to my wife, Caroline, who coped alone with three children for eleven years, keeping a household going and yet still finding the time to support me when needed, that our three boys have turned out to be perfectly stable and upright members of society. Thankfully they do not take after their father in their behaviour and, if they read this book, I hope I can live down the resultant, and quite justified, mickey taking.

Please, do enjoy the book for what it is, a comic selection of episodes from life at sea.

I have changed all the names to protect the guilty but, if any of my old crew mates should recognise themselves, all I can say is, you shouldn't have done it in the first place, should you?

—Chas Cooke

I must go down to the sea again,
To the lonely shore and the sky,
I left my pants and socks on a rock,
I do hope the buggers are dry.

This book is dedicated to my wife, Caroline, in constant admiration of the hardships she endured whilst I was at sea, left to bring up our children alone coping with the absence of the one person she should have been able to rely on to be there when she needed him.

Me.

CHAPTER ONE

"Right, that's your joining routine done, you can make your way down to the ship then."

The Regulating Petty Officer nodded in the general direction of the dockyard.

"Which one is the Ark Royal then P.O.?" I asked, looking into the rain and gloom in the direction of his nod.

"You can't miss it son, it's down there."

"Is it behind that block of flats then?" I asked, hoping for a little more help than he seemed willing to give.

"That's not flats boy, that is Ark Royal."

"Bloody hell!" I gawped at the huge shape with lights all over it about half a mile away down the hill. Not a block of flats? That had to be one big ship. All my training so far had been on world war two destroyers and Leander class frigates destined for the scrap heap. I had no idea that they made ships that big.

I hauled my kit bag onto my shoulder, hoisted my naval issue suitcase off the ground and trudged away toward the dockyard. I had been in the navy for ten months and I had filled out my first ever drafting preference card six months ago. It was supposed to be my opportunity to select the type of ship and the port in which I preferred to spend my next two years. It was obviously not for that reason at all. The form was clearly meant to give the naval drafting office the opportunity to have a good laugh and be as sadistic as possible. I had, in good faith and with the innocence of youth, asked to serve in a Portsmouth based minesweeper. And here I was, my very first ship, fifty thousand tons of aircraft carrier based in Plymouth. Someone must have been laughing like a drain somewhere in an office in Gosport. Bastard.

After what seemed like miles of dark, wet, slippery roads, dockyard railway lines designed to trip the unwary and numerous trips into dead ends where dry docks were open and roads closed, I finally stood on a jetty, littered with a mountain of stores and equipment, looking up at the one hundred and twenty feet of Ark Royal which filled the gap between the water and the flight deck. Surely it wasn't floating, It was too big.

I looked along the jetty in both directions and spotted a gangway about half a mile away, or so it seemed. Sweating, I hauled my kit bag and case to the foot of the wooden ramp and dragged myself to the top.

"What do you think you're doing?"

I looked up to see an immaculately dressed Lieutenant Commander, with a brass telescope under his left arm. Beside him was a similarly immaculately uniformed Leading Seaman. I tried to straighten up under my load, looking more like a pack mule than a sailor.

"I'm joining the ship sir."

"Not here you're not young man."

He must have seen the puzzled look on my face. What was he on about?

"This is the officer's gangway, the ratings' gangway is aft, down there." He walked to the rail and pointed along the jetty.

I followed his finger and, in the far distance, I could just see another chain of lights joining the jetty to a point halfway up the side of the ship.

I turned around and, swearing under my breath, struggled down the gangway, slipping and stumbling on the wet wood. It took me fifteen minutes to walk to the other gangway and I arrived, sweating and disheveled in front of a large Chief Petty Officer.

"Who are we then?"

"Junior Electrician Cooke," I replied. "I'm joining the ship."

"Ah yes, right, you're in four lima two mess. We've been expecting you. You're bloody late."

"My train was delayed at Exeter Chief, I got here as quickly as I could."

"Well, you've missed supper, maybe you can get a cup of tea in the mess."

"Where is four lima two mess please chief?"

Once again, a finger was waved. "Follow that passageway until you come to the officer's gangway and the door is right next to the top of it."

I looked at him. Someone was taking the piss here. I set off and having reached the immaculate Lieutenant Commander again, I found the door. The bastard was standing right in front of it. I'm sure he was grinning as I kicked the door open and tried to get through without ripping the frame away with my kitbag and case.

Inside, the air was hot and a thick mist of cigarette smoke filled the mess. A sailor sitting on one of the seats formed by the foldaway bunks looked up at me over the can of beer held in his right hand.

"Yeah. Can we help you?"

I introduced myself and explained that I was the new member of the mess.

"Oh. Cooke. Right. Did you know you're duty tonight?"

"But I can't be, it's my first night."

"Look, it says so on Daily Orders." He handed me a sheet of printed paper with the ship's crest on the top and as I looked down the sheet, there, under the heading, Duty Electrical Ratings, was my name. I couldn't believe this. First night on the ship, late arriving after a nightmare journey from Portsmouth, sweaty, knackered and hungry and already I was duty.

A television was perched on a shelf above a bank of grey steel kit lockers. The phone beneath the television was ringing. A hand reached out from a nearby bunk and the handset disappeared behind the curtain shielding the occupant from view. A few seconds later the hand reappeared, still holding the handset and a voice bellowed from behind the curtain.

"Switchboard for some twat called Cooke. Anyone know him?"

I looked around in the vain hope that perhaps there may be another Cooke in the mess. As usual today, I was sorely disappointed and I took the handset from the fingers protruding from the curtains.

"Hello." I said, weakly.

"Is that JEM Cooke?"

"Yes."

"Get your arse down to the main switchboard, we've got a job for you."

"Where is the switchboard?"

"6NZO." There followed a click as the handset at the other end was replaced in its cradle.

I turned to the man with the beer.

"That was the switchboard, they said they had a job for me. What do I do?"

He leant to one side, looking past me at the television and replied,

"You get your arse down the switchboard and do whatever job they give you to do. Now get out of the way of the tele, you're blocking my view of Pan's People."

I dumped my kitbag and case in a suitable corner of the mess and headed off in search of the switchboard. 6NZO, that's six deck, November section, at the aft end of that section and on the ship's centreline. Easy.

Two hours later and I finally, almost by accident, managed to find the switchboard. The ship was huge. Fourteen decks below the flight deck, as long as four football pitches and as wide as a football pitch is long, and I felt as though I had been over every inch of that ship. I lost count of the ladders I had climbed and the doorways I had passed through. My shins were bruised and grazed from the raised steel door lips and my calves and thighs ached from climbing and descending the ladders. I went in to find two electrical ratings sitting at a large desk on a raised platform. In front of them was a curved display covered in lights and symbols, which showed the layout of the main electrical generating system on the ship. Just at a quick glance I could see the symbols for ten generators.

"What do you want?"

I looked at the speaker and noticed the name tape on his shirt, 'Sherman'.

"I'm Cooke. You phoned me in the mess and told me you had a job."

"That was two bleedin' hours ago. Where have you been?"

I launched into an explanation of the problems I had experienced in navigating my way around the ship. I had managed three words when I was cut off in full flow. It was Sherman speaking again.

"Never mind that crap. Someone else had to do that job."

I must have looked relieved because he gave a rather sickly grin.

"Don't you worry, we've got another job for you. This one's been waiting ages. Nobody else wanted to do it."

He handed me a printed work sheet. Scruffy handwriting spread across the page. 'Bilge pump, B boiler room. Buggered.' it said.

He reached down under the desk and handed me a grey oilskin electrician's tool roll.

"You'd better get a shimmy on son, the stokers'll have a right toot on by now."

I asked for directions to B boiler room and, as seemed to be normal behaviour on this ship, a limp finger was waved, vaguely in the direction of the door.

"It's out there—somewhere." He said, and with that picked up a girly magazine, put his feet on the desk and ignored me.

Now, HMS Ark Royal had four engine rooms, four boiler rooms, four gear rooms, four plumber blocks and four shaft spaces. I should have known the way this would turn out. It had just been one of those days. I found nineteen of the twenty possible places that could have been B boiler room. When, on the twentieth attempt, I got to the right one I could have cried. Standing there at the hatch leading down into the steamy, noisy, claustrophobic boiler room, I glanced behind me. Through the door, immediately next to the boiler room hatch, I could see Sherman, in the switchboard, sitting with his feet still on the desk and his girly magazine still in his hand. I had walked what seemed like miles, only to end up three feet from where I had started.

I looked down through the hatch to the boiler room below. It was like a scene from Hades. Pipes seemed to weave a tangled web around the area I could see. Sweating men stood around with ear protectors on. The noise, even from outside, was deafening. I carefully climbed down the ladder into the boiler room. As I descended, the area opened up before me. It was huge but every spare space seemed to be filled with pipe work or gauges. Steam burst out of every corner. On a steel platform, before a huge bank of gleaming brass gauges, stood several men in dark blue overalls.

"Excuse me!" I shouted trying to make myself heard above the din. It had no effect. I may as well have not been there. I moved forward and tapped one of them on the shoulder. He looked at me and raised his eyebrows. I showed him the worksheet, which he took from me to read. He handed it back and walked off, beckoning for me to follow. He led me through a maze of pipes and down a mass of ladders and then stopped abruptly in front of me. He waved for me to come closer and, as I looked over his shoulder, he pointed below us to what was obviously a pump of some kind. He looked at me and walked away, leaving me alone.

The pump was covered in grease and slime. I could see the hull of the ship nearby. I was at the very bottom of this huge ship and expected to climb into the greasy, filthy bilges. There, up to my knees in water covered in an oily scum, I was supposed to delve my fingers into a pump containing live electrical components. I couldn't help myself, I burst out laughing.

I carefully climbed into the cold water, unrolled my tool roll and selected the biggest hammer I could find and hit the pump casing as hard as I could. A large crack appeared and water began to seep through from the inside. Replacing the hammer, I rolled up the tool kit and made my way back up the ladders. As I passed the men standing on the platform I smiled and gave them a thumbs up.

Leaving the boiler room, I walked into the switchboard and threw the tool roll into Sherman's lap. It seemed to sink into his scrotum and his feet fell off the desk as he grasped his testicles, going red in the face.

"It's not an electrical problem with that pump. It's mechanical. The casings cracked. You'd better get a stoker to look at it." I said, and, grinning, walked out of the switchboard and made my way back to the mess for a cup of tea.

What a way to start your first day on your first ship.

CHAPTER TWO

A loudspeaker next to my ear was bellowing. I looked out from under my sheets. I was in the top bunk of four. People were moving about the mess in various states of undress and a cacophony of farting and belching echoed around the living space. From my lofty view I could see several men energetically scratching their testicles. I sat up and smashed the top of my head into the steel pipe that ran along the top of my bunk. Someone with a towel wrapped round his waist helpfully pointed out that I should 'Mind that pipe.' So, this was where I would live for the foreseeable future. Still, at least I had a good view of the tele from up here.

I carefully climbed out of my bunk and made my way down to deck level. I had been allocated a locker and had spent some time the previous night trying to cram all my kit into it. I had given up after an hour and left a host of items, which I didn't think I would need immediately, in my kit bag that had then been stowed in a large storage space at the far end of the mess.

I followed the example of others and helped myself to a mug of tea from the large water boiler in the corner. My towel was hanging on the rail at the front of my locker and, needing a shower, I picked it up and headed along the passageway, to where I had been told the toilets and showers were situated. There were bodies moving around everywhere I looked, most of them with towels around their waists, some of them were even stark bollock naked. I waited my turn for a vacant shower and, feeling refreshed headed back to the mess to dress for breakfast.

The dining hall was two decks above, and right at the bows of the ship. It was massive, dwarfed only by the queue of sailors fighting for egg and bacon served on steel trays. The noise level would have made Status Quo flinch as 2500 men ate and talked.

I finished my meal and, with the help of several sets of directions, most of which were totally wrong, made my way to my new work place, the bomb lift section on 6 deck. There were three bomb lifts on the ship. They were used to move ammunition from the magazines on 12 deck up to the waiting aircraft on the flight deck. Each bomb lift consisted of two hoists. The first carried the bombs and missiles from 12 deck, up 6 levels to 6 deck. There, they were taken off of the hoist, moved across a transfer space and placed on another hoist which carried them the remainder of the way, a further 6 levels to the flight deck. This prevented the chance of a flight deck fire ever having a direct path into the magazines, a fatal condition for a ship carrying as much explosive as the Ark Royal. Hydraulically operated steel shutters, also designed to be fire and flash proof protected each hoist.

Two of the lifts shared the same transfer space toward the front of the ship; the third lift was aft. In a corner of the forward transfer space was a cramped office where I was introduced to my new boss, Chief Petty Officer Scott. He was a large, unsmiling man who seemed to chain smoke small but extremely evil smelling cigars.

"So you're the new lad then." He said, more in the form of a statement than a question. "Right, we'd better find you a sea daddy, hadn't we?"

"A what, Chief?" I enquired.

"All the new boys have a sea daddy." He explained. "They help you find your way around and show you a few of the ropes to get you started."

I thought that I could have done with somebody like that the previous night but thought better of saying anything. I remembered the advice given at training school, keep your ears and eyes open, your mouth shut, smile and say yes. I smiled and said "Yes Chief."

"Right, let's see who we can give you to."

I thought it sounded as though I was to be sold into homosexual slavery the way he said it but, eyes and ears open, mouth shut. The Chief looked past me and he smiled.

"Just the man. George, I want you to be young Cooke's sea daddy for the next few weeks."

I looked round and, to my horror, came face to face with a nametape bearing the word 'Sherman'. I looked up and into the face of the man whose scrotum I had so badly mistreated in the main switchboard the night before. He had a nose that looked as though it was made of putty, moulded by an insane glazier. He had obviously been in a few fist fights in his time, and if he had won them I would have hated to see the poor bugger that lost.

"Oh shit." I looked around to see who had spoken and realised, by the way everyone was looking at me, that the words must have come from my mouth.

"Morning George." I said, holding out my hand, "Chas Cooke, I think we met last night."

Yes, we did, didn't we?" He said grasping my hand in his. I looked down and I swear he'd lost a hand in the past and had a transplant from an orangutang. His hand was massive and covered in dark red hair. It was also very strong as the crack of the bones in my hand testified.

"Oh good, so you two are friends already then." Said the Chief as he lit yet another foul smelling cigar.

I could see that life on the Ark Royal was going to be…interesting.

My first experience of instruction, under the guidance of George Sherman was a revelation. Eight o' clock in the morning and, as usual,

I reported to the office in the bomb transfer space. It was there that Chief Scott handed out all the job sheets detailing the work to be completed that day. George and I had settled our differences very quickly and actually got on very well. George was handed a sheet, which he read and handed over to me. The defect we were tasked with rectifying was a lighting circuit in a small machinery room. It had been blowing fuses for the last few days and was causing problems to the men trying to work in the area. George and I trudged off, down ladders and through cramped passageways until we came to the relevant machine room. It was in darkness. On the bulkheads were steel plates which listed all the electrical circuits in the area and which fuse panel fed each circuit. I found the relevant legend for the lighting circuit and, while George sat in a corner, next to a small generator which was blowing out warm air, smoking a cigarette, I hauled my reluctant body back up three ladders to the fuse box. There I removed the fuses for the lighting circuit before returning to the machine room. I found George, still in the comer and fast asleep. I shook him gently and he slowly came to.

"The fuses are out, George."

"Right Chas, how do you fix this then?" he asked.

I cast my mind back to training school.

"I'll use the test leads and check for earth. If there is an earth, that will be the problem. I can then start breaking the circuit down until I find out which component is causing the problem and replace it."

"Bollocks!"

I was sure I was right. Perhaps I had forgotten all the training I had received. I must have been in the wrong lesson when they taught us this bit.

"I'm sure that's the way you do it."

"Take me to the fuse panel and I'll show you what to do." George demanded.

Once again I wended my merry way back to the fuse box with George, gasping and wheezing behind me.

"This is the one, George, it's the circuit with the fuses out."

"Right, hang onto this and get ready to run." He handed me a black, carbon dioxide filled fire extinguisher, the type used especially for fires in electrical equipment. "Give me your tool roll and mind your eyes."

I watched in amazement as he unrolled the tool kit, removed a large hammer and without hesitating slammed the head of the hammer across the contacts normally spanned by the fuses protecting the circuit.

"Right, leg it, back to the machine room." He said and set off at, what for George, was quite a reasonable gallop. He didn't touch the steps as he went back down the ladders. He slid down the rails on his hands with his feet in the air, taking an entire ladder in one leap. I struggled to keep up with him. I was trying to hang on to the tool roll and the fire extinguisher. We burst back into the machine room, which was strangely lit. I looked into the space and noticed that there was an acrid smell of hot electrical insulation and smoke in the air. George pointed to a light fitting in the far corner, which was ablaze and dripping melting plastic on the deck.

"That's the bugger there," he said, "Put the fire out and when it's cooled down we'll change it for a new one." And with that he settled back down on the deck and lit another cigarette.

It was shortly after this that the Ark Royal brought home to me how tenuous our hold on life really is. I was sixteen years old; only just old enough to get my duty free cigarettes but not yet old enough to drink when I saw my first death. An aircraft carrier is, they say, the most dangerous workplace on earth. It was proved to be so one morning.

The bomb lifts were contained within a normal lift shaft. Each lift had it's own set of keys and the key had to be placed into a lock on an electrical power supply box and turned to allow the lift to operate. All the time that the key was in the lock, safety interlocks prevented the doors into the lift shafts from being opened. Of course, at sea, if the keys were lost the lift would be out of action if no spare were carried. The keys were drawn each day from HQ1, the damage control centre, and signed for by the recipient. One of the bomb lift staff went to start the lift one morning but the keys were missing and had not been signed

22

for. It was assumed that they had been lost and a spare set was issued. What had in fact happened was that someone had taken the keys earlier, but forgot to sign them out. He had entered the lift shaft to carry out maintenance and was working inside when the second, spare set of keys were used to start the lift. As the lift descended toward him the man in the shaft panicked. His first action should have been to drop to the bottom of the lift shaft where a painted area was marked on the deck. If one lay on the painted area the lift would stop on its limits leaving enough room for one person to lie beneath it without being crushed. In his panic the man tried desperately to climb the ladder to the exit door in the side of the shaft. He was too slow and, still some distance short of the door, the lift hit him on the back of the head. This alone did not kill him. His legs slipped through the rungs of the ladder and he was hanging there, with the rung caught behind his knees and the entire weight of the lift now on his back. He was bent double and the lift had canted in its runners causing it to jam. Slowly the lift crept down, crushing him still further. His cries were heard and, despite attempts to raise the lift it would not move in any direction except slowly down.

The ship's doctors were called and while they did their best to keep him alive a crane on the flight deck was used to try to lift the platform off the man. People were desperately working as fast as they could, but to no avail. I recall to this day that, as the sound of his bones cracking echoed in the lift shaft, the tears streamed down the doctor's cheeks. There was nothing to be done and the young man died in the shaft.

The atmosphere among the bomb lift crews was muted for days. Safety procedures were updated but all too late for one young life.

CHAPTER THREE

Overall, my time on the Ark was good. The ship was full of personalities and there was always room for a practical joke and a laugh.

While alongside in Plymouth, during a maintenance period, the steam catapults were due for testing. Each of the two catapults, operated by steam pressure, were powerful enough to throw a buccaneer or phantom aircraft weighing many tons, from zero to 130 miles per hour in less than a second. Their power was immense.

To test these catapults, dead weights were used. These were massive metal blocks bolted onto a Canberra bomber undercarriage. They were strapped to the catapult and flung over the bows of the ship. The resultant splash, as they hit the water some one hundred and twenty feet below, was impressive to say the least. One morning, during the testing, a notice appeared on the ship's notice board asking for volunteers to act as Dead Load Pilots. Unbelievably they received several applications from the greener and more gullible members of the crew. A series of tests were introduced, including a full medical for each of the unfortunate victims of the hoax. Each hopeful applicant was paraded before the Captain to give his reasons for being selected. The

Commander Flying interviewed all at length and the lucky appointee was kitted out in full flying suit before being briefed on his mission.

On a hot sunny day, in front of most of the crew, who had gathered at the rear of the flight deck to watch him make a fool of himself, the lucky man was brought out to meet his challenge. A tubular steel chair was dumped unceremoniously on top of the dead weight and the man, I have to say he was a stoker, was helped up into the chair. His visor was lowered and his lifejacket and oxygen mask were checked. Surely he would soon realise that this was a wind up. The catapult crew asked him if he was happy and, with a jolly smile and a thumbs up he braced himself for the flight.

At this point a temporary halt was called to the proceedings. He was taken from the chair and led to the bow of the ship to watch a launch. He stood proudly at the front of the flight deck and watched as the dead weight hurtled down the flight deck and disappeared into oblivion. The splash soaked him and those standing by him. The tubular chair, which had been on top of the dead weight, lay forlornly bent and mangled back at the launch point.

"What do you reckon then? Still want to go ahead with it?" He was asked.

"Oh yes." He replied. "I don't think the flying is a problem. I may have a little trouble with the landing, but I'm willing to give it a go."

The flight deck erupted with the laughter of two thousand men and the unfortunate victim was unceremoniously bundled below where an explanation followed. Unluckily for him, it didn't just end there. The story was leaked to "Navy News", the Royal Navy's own newspaper, and was spread around the entire fleet. How do you live that down when you are seventeen and have 23 years of naval service to look forward to?

My time on Ark Royal was coming to an end. I had enjoyed my time onboard and was not looking forward to going ashore. Although it was a huge ship in which you could become lost and anonymous, it was, overall, a very happy ship. There was always something to do. The

Royal Marine Band gave concerts on the quarterdeck, the flight deck, when not in use for flying, gave ample room for sports and, being so big, there was always somewhere one could go to get away from the rest of the crew. My favourite spot was just below the flight deck on the port side. A ladder led from the flight deck to a metal grating, which then allowed access to the deck below. Sitting on the grating, a hundred feet above the water was like flying alongside the ship. I could see above and below me and I could look along the entire length of the ship as its fifty thousand tons hurled itself through the water at thirty knots.

Six levels above the flight deck, on the island, was the rocket launcher deck. Next to the funnel and sheltered from the wind it was an ideal sunbathing spot. Even on a cold blustery day the heat from the metal of the funnel would keep me comfortably warm. I spent many happy hour after work, sitting there, watching the world go by.

The Ark, as its crew affectionately knew the ship, was the Royal Navy's pride and joy. It was the biggest ship they owned and, whenever possible they showed it off to the world. Fort Lauderdale, Florida was a favourite run ashore for the crew and the whole ship eagerly looked forward to a forthcoming visit. The trouble with a ship that size is that the crew, all 2500 of them, tend to swamp the port of call and stretch the host town's hospitality to the limit. The Americans seemed to have thought of that one and, on arrival a telephone hotline was installed. Local families could phone the ship and "order" a sailor or two to take home for the day and show them the sights of the area. In general this was a good idea that worked well, however, it did tend to leave the system open to abuse. I recall seeing one young sailor waiting for his host at the gangway when a large pink motorcar purred to a halt on the jetty. Out of this vehicle appeared an apparition in pink and white who minced his way to the top of the gangway with his white toy poodle under his arm and announced to all within earshot, "I'm here to claim my sailor for the day". He gave the name of his allotted victim and the young, blonde haired, blue-eyed sailor was last seen hurtling along the weather deck, protectively clenching his buttocks.

The crew as a whole tended to spend such runs ashore in an alcoholic daze. The naval clothing store was at its busiest on such visits due to the amount of uniform clothing lost, sold or given away for sexual favours.

During my trip to America on the Ark, I was sitting on the beach sunning myself and enjoying the warm Florida sun. It seemed that half the crew were on the beach that day, most of them in various stages of drunkenness and a good proportion of them accompanied by young American females. Not five yards from me, a large, bearded seaman was practicing what, in the navy, is known as Egyptian Gymnastics or counterpane hurdling. His white tropical uniform trousers were around his ankles and his bare arse was pumping up and down to the obvious delight of the young woman buried somewhere under his voluminous beer gut. I was hypnotised by the sight and was amazed to see a slender hand emerge from under him and reach for a can of Coca Cola, which was sitting on the sand. I nearly died of apoplexy when, in an American drawl, the young woman, in between sips of drink, said to the now sweating sailor,

"Do you think you could get your balls in as well? You're flicking sand up my arse".

The visit to America ended all too soon and, as a year had passed since I joined the ship, my next posting had been decided. I was to return to HMS Collingwood, the naval electrical training school as ship's company. No longer a trainee, I would be subject to less harsh discipline and certainly have an easier time there then I had whilst under training. Still, I would miss the Ark Royal. There were rumours that it was soon to be scrapped and I felt myself privileged to have been part of her crew. With her own Chinese laundry, Chinese tailors, post office, supermarket and even a cobblers making hand made shoes, she was an impressive piece of seagoing hardware. I was walking along the passageway back to the mess, considering my future after Ark Royal. I bumped into someone coming the other way.

"Watch where you're bloody going." I said and lifted my head to see who this clumsy oaf was. I was astounded. It was Jeff Shelwood. I had joined with Jeff nearly two years earlier and, since I had left training to join Ark Royal, we had not seen each other.

"Jeff. You old tart. How are you doing?"

"Chas, Jeez, I didn't know you were on here, have you just joined?"

I looked at him puzzled. "No, I've been on here for a year, I'm leaving next week to go back to Collingwood. I thought you'd just joined the ship."

"No Chas, I've been on here for six months."

It was a graphic example of the size of the ship we were serving in. Six months we had been aboard together and had never bumped into each other in the entire time. On a ship that size it was normal to become friendly with those whose mess deck you shared and those with whom you worked. Outside of that circle faces blurred into one another and became lost. It was, in fact, like living in a large housing estate of 600 homes, each containing four or five people. It was impossible to know every single person and friendships were few and far between. In a housing estate you do not have the added problem of ten percent of the estate moving out and a new ten percent taking their place every few months.

I hoped that my next sea going posting would be to a somewhat smaller class of ship. If I had only known just how small my next ship would be, perhaps I would have kept my thoughts to myself.

CHAPTER FOUR

I strolled through the gates of HMS Collingwood, proudly wearing my cap with HMS Ark Royal emblazoned on the cap tally. I was a salty sea dog now, these young sprogs under training would look up to me and see me for what I was, a well travelled experienced rating of the Royal Navy.

"Oy! Come here you little shit."

I chuckled to myself; some poor trainee was going to get a hard time. I was glad that no one would talk to me like that, now that I was experienced.

"Are you bloody deaf you ginger haired tosspot?"

I looked around to watch the fun. It was worth coming back to a shore establishment to see the trainees getting it in the neck.

"If you don't come over here and report to me in the next ten seconds I will personally rip your head off and shit in your neck before tearing off one of your arms and beating you to death with the soggy end."

Two things suddenly dawned on me. One, I was the only person in the vicinity and, two, the mouth with a uniform on was pointing at me. It was a Master at Arms, a chief petty officer of the Naval Regulating Branch, the Royal Navy's version of the Military Police.

"Yes, you Einstein."

He is shouting at me. Oh well, these little misunderstandings will occur from time to time. I'm sure he'll change when he sees my Ark Royal cap tally and realises that I'm not some little trainee.

I strolled across to him and he looked me up and down with an expression that intimated that someone had strapped a dog turd under his nose.

"And who the hell are we then?"

"I'm Junior Ordnance Electrical Mechanic Cooke, Chief." I replied with a smile. I waited for him to spot the cap tally and invite me into his office for a chat about life at sea and a cup of tea. I was to be cruelly disappointed.

"Don't call me bleedin' Chief."

I refrained from asking him for his first name when I spotted the slight tremor of his upper lip and the sweat beginning to bead upon his brow.

"Sorry Master." I said, opting instead to address him by his proper title. "I'm just joining ship's company from HMS Ark Royal."

Again I expected the light to dawn upon him; surely he must realise that I was no green little trainee to be bawled at from dawn to dusk.

"Well, I don't know what the rules were in regard to haircuts on the Ark Royal, but in my establishment you do not walk through the main gate looking like the tart out of Peters and Lee. You will report to me at 1200 hours having had a haircut, in your best uniform and with your shoes polished. Do you understand me?"

"Yes Master."

It was obvious that I had been under some delusion about my own standing in the Royal Navy. Didn't this man know that I had been to sea for a year, on the Royal Navy's biggest and most powerful ship? Perhaps it was jealousy. I decided that it would be best not to antagonise him further and meekly slunk away to carry out my joining routine. I could feel his eyes boring into my back as I walked away from the main gate. First stop, the barbers. Oh bugger! I thought this was going to be a holiday camp, it would appear to be more like a prison camp.

Life calmed down for a while after my introduction to life ashore. I was given a cushy little job in one of the Chief Petty Officer's messes. My life consisted of making sure the bar was tidy and the glasses washed up before sitting down for the remainder of the day, watching tele and reading the newspaper. This was more like it. Then, someone decided to build one big Senior Rates Mess and staff it with civilian stewards. All the little wooden huts dotted around the base, and used as messes, were closed and I was, in a funny sort of way, unemployed. In situations like this fate always takes a hand. I hoped for another, equally cushy number, somewhere quiet and out of harms way, but oh no, not me. Some sadistic sod decided that I would be usefully employed as a sentry at the main gate. That meant working shifts, alternate hours spent standing outside the gate in a sentry box checking car and security passes. And guess who the man in charge was: Yes, my mate the Master at Arms. My life was becoming a misery and I would have to put up with it until the naval drafting office decided where I was to go next.

"Here, Chas, I've got a draft."

I looked round. It was Paddy, one of the other main gate sentries on my watch. We had arrived at the same time, both after our first spell at sea.

"You didn't look to see if I've got one did you?" I asked hopefully.

He held out a piece of paper in his hand with a grin. Oh deep joy. I was being released.

"Have you opened yours yet, Paddy?"

"No, not yet."

We ripped open the envelopes and Paddy's face fell. His jaw went slack and a glazed look came over him.

"They must be joking, submarines. What the heck do I want to go and live under water for? It's dangerous, I could be hurt or seriously killed."

I wasn't so keen to look at mine now. If Paddy was being sent to the submarine service, I could be going with him. I looked at the name of the ship on the form and a feeling of relief washed over me.

"What have you got then?"

I tried not to look as though I was gloating. "HMS Norfolk, one of the new guided missile destroyers, okay I suppose." I said.

"I don't suppose you want to swap do you?" Paddy pleaded.

"You must be joking. I've got a mate on the Norfolk, it'll be great."

Paddy turned and walked away. Even from the back he looked worried. His shoulders drooped and his boots scraped on the road with each step he took. I walked inside and let out the grin that had been bursting to get free.

Later that evening I managed to find a few minutes free to phone the Norfolk, which was currently undergoing a short maintenance period alongside in Portsmouth.

"Dave, it's Chas Cooke, yeah, great thanks. Here, I've just got my draft chit and guess where I'm going. No, not Colchester Military Prison, I'm coming to join the Norfolk with you. Yeah it's brilliant isn't it? When? In six weeks. Poor old Paddy has got submarines. Yeah, I'm glad it's him and not me. What's the Norfolk like? That good eh? Under eighteen, yes, I'm still under eighteen. I'm only just turned seventeen, why? You what? PT! On the flight deck. Before breakfast. What, every bloody morning? How long for? A whole bleedin' hour. Oh my god, I hate exercise, I break out in sweats and breathlessness. Yeah, alright mate, see you soon, cheers."

I put the phone down. PT on the flight deck, every morning until I'm eighteen. Oh God. I hate physical exercise. I even played in goal in the school football team so I didn't have to run round like a lunatic. Oh God. What was I going to do now?

"Alright Paddy?"

"Alright Chas."

Three hours later and I was in the mess sitting on a chair, looking at Paddy sprawled on his bed, the very picture of abject misery. I handed him two pieces of paper, naval request forms, one made out in his name and one made out in mine, the latter signed by me. He read the forms and leapt off the bed.

"Give me a bloody pen, quick, before you change your mind."

He grabbed the biro from my hand, scrawled his signature on the form with his name on it and ran from the room with indecent haste. I began to think that, perhaps, I had made a bit of a faux pas. The request forms I had handed over to him were asking permission for the two of us to swap drafts. If approved, I would go to submarines while Paddy went to the Norfolk and did the PT. This may give you some idea of just how much I detested physical exercise. Still there was always the chance that the officer in charge of drafting would refuse the request. Yes, and hell was just about to freeze over. Two weeks later and a new draft chit arrived. I was going to the submarine service and Paddy was going to the Norfolk. Then I realized, I hadn't seen Paddy since the day I had handed him the request forms. I never saw him again. There's bloody gratitude for you.

With twenty-four hours to go before I left Collingwood and joined Captain Nemo's mates twenty thousand leagues under the sea, my mate the Master at Arms struck again.

"Cooke, get in my sodding office, now!"

I followed the direction of the bawl, along the passageway, to the Master at Arms office.

"You screamed for me Master?"

"Don't get sarcastic Cooke. You may be going to join those horrible smelly submariners after tomorrow, but today you are still a member of my main gate staff. I've noticed your hair is getting a bit long again. Haircut muster is at 1000 hours tomorrow morning and you will be there. We can't have you leaving here like that can we? Your hair is long enough to put in a ponytail and there's only one thing you can be sure of when it comes to ponytails. Every time you lift one up to have a look, there's always an arsehole underneath it. Report to me tomorrow with nice short hair."

I left his office.

My final watch on the main gate was the following afternoon. I started just as the Master at Arms finished. Quickly I put on my gaiters and armband and took first spell on the gate. From the sentry box I could see the Master at Arms leaving his office and climbing into his car. As he approached the gate I left the sentry box to lift the barrier. I walked just slowly enough that he had to stop his car and wait. As I lifted the barrier I took off my cap and let my uncut hair fall over my ears. Just for effect I flicked it off of my face with a casual toss of the head. I thought he would explode. His face was a deep beetroot red and his eyes were beginning to water.

"COOKE! I thought I told you to attend the barbers and get your hair cut."

I sauntered across to the driver's window, leant on the door and looked him in the face.

"Oh, I'm bloody sorry, I must've missed the muster, Master."

I turned and walked back to my sentry box. I could hear little gurglings and gasps coming from the car. I turned, gave him a cheery wave and stepped back into the small hut. With a squeal of tyres, his car hurtled off down the street. I burst out laughing. Goodbye Collingwood and up you Master, right up you!

CHAPTER FIVE

"Good morning gentlemen. Before you on the desk you will see a number of forms that you need to fill out. While you do that I'm going for a smoke, I'll be back in twenty minutes."

With that, the Petty Officer turned and walked out of the room. I looked around me and saw there were twenty or so other men of varying ages in the room. I was probably the youngest and, at seventeen, I didn't even have to be there. The Navy could make a sailor join the submarine service but, until he was eighteen, he could only be sent to sea on one if he volunteered. Like a complete idiot, I had done just that. I looked down at the pile of papers in front of me. The first one in the pile was that old favourite, the drafting preference card. I cynically filled it out with all the details of the submarine I would least like to serve on. Using reverse logic would mean that I was bound to be sent to the type that I really did want to go to, diesel submarines. I didn't even know the names of any nuclear submarines so, in that box, I simply wrote, 'I will leave this one to you'.

I moved the drafting preference card to one side and looked at the next form. Last Will and Testament—Naval Will Form. What the hell? Hang on a minute, I haven't even started my training and, already, they were actually expecting me to die horribly, suffocating in a submarine thousands of feet below the sea. I began to wonder what I had let myself in for.

I had three months of training ahead of me. First I had to complete the basic submarine course, how a submarine moves, fights, dives and, most importantly of all, surfaces again. There seemed to be a baffling amount to learn about trim tanks, hydroplanes, periscopes, pressures and safety procedures. I worked hard and came to the last week of the basic course, submarine escape. To a man, everyone on the course was dreading this bit. It was our first opportunity to drown whilst in the submarine service.

If you have ever sailed out of Portsmouth on a ferry to the Isle of Wight or France, you will probably have noticed that, on the foreshore of the Gosport side of the Solent, is a very tall square tower. It is just over a hundred feet high and, though you can't see it from the outside, it is full of water. This is the submarine escape training tank, or SETT. This was where submariners trained to escape from their stricken submarines. After a series of briefings, which included time in a recompression chamber, to check for problems with the ears which may occur at depth, the real business of practical training began. Dressed in issued yellow swimming trunks and a bathrobe, and having watched a brief demonstration by an instructor, the victims, namely myself and the twenty-three other pale and nervous sailors, were taken down from the top of the tower to the thirty-foot level. Here, we were taken inside and the big, watertight, door shut behind us. The space was flooded and, with just a small air space at the top in which to breathe, the door into the main tower was opened. One at a time we shuffled our way to the opening into the tower. Soon it was my turn. Round my waist was a webbing belt with two small tabs at the back. On the command of the instructor, "Take a good deep breath." I did just that. My head was pushed down under the water and my backside, as a result, stuck through the opening. Two swimmer instructors pulled me through the small door and into the tank. There I was, thirty feet below the surface and seventy feet above the bottom, with no other air than that in my lungs. The instructors held me there until they could be sure that, as instructed, I was slowly blowing air out through my mouth. They finally let me go and, very, very slowly, I began to float upwards. I began to panic. I was going to run out of air long before I got to the top. Then I realised, what they had told me was true. As the water pressure on my body decreased the air in my lungs began to expand. I had plenty of air left. I began to enjoy myself until, finally, after what seemed an age, I sedately broke the surface and took a fresh lungful of air. I couldn't wait to do it again. In the true tradition of the service, it had to be proved that the first time was not a fluke. We were taken down to repeat the procedure. Another run from thirty feet, followed by an ascent from sixty feet and, finally, the ultimate thrill, the same from a hundred feet. It was great. I could have gone on all day. The final test was another ascent from a hundred feet, this time in a suit. It was like a personal life raft, which, on arrival at the surface would inflate around the body to keep you afloat. A hood went over the head and upper chest and a life jacket in the suit was inflated. As I flew toward the surface the air in the lifejacket expanded and the excess was allowed to escape into the hood. This in turn inflated and allowed me to breathe normally as I rushed through the water. I reached the surface so quickly that my entire body came out of the water before splashing back into it like a bright orange whale. What a thrill. It was probably the most enjoyable part of the basic submarine course and all the sweeter as it meant I was now qualified to receive special service allowance, submarine pay, a massive one pound forty-four pence per day. I was rich and I was going to enjoy my new found wealth.

CHAPTER SIX

It was toward the end of the basic submarine training that the naval drafting office decided which class of submarine we would be sent to. It would appear that I was not the first person to try the old reverse logic trick. I had been rumbled. I wanted to go to diesel submarines and had deliberately, as you may recall, asked to go to nuclear hunter killer class. They were too good for me. They had obviously seen through my ploy. They had actually given me what I asked for. I was going to be subjected to radiation. I would be sterile, I would never have children, my hair would fall out and I would glow in the dark. Still, I suppose that would save on torch batteries when I wanted to read in bed.

The decision having been made we were split into four smaller groups. There was a group for each class of submarine. Diesel electric, Swiftsure class hunter killer, Valiant class hunter killer and Resolution class Polaris missile submarines. I was to join Her Majesty's Submarine Courageous, a Valiant Repeat class nuclear powered hunter killer. With a crew of about one hundred and ten, it was a medium sized boat. Really, I was quite looking forward to it. The nuclear boats got some good runs ashore and, unlike the diesel boats, they had a few of the comforts of a normal life.

For the next few weeks I spent hours in the classroom and, even after instruction was complete for the day, my bedtime reading consisted mainly of technical sheets giving details of hydraulic, water, air and various other systems required to make a submarine work. I did, of course, browse through the occasional Mayfair and Playgirl for a little light relief, but the less said about that the better I should think.

HMS Dolphin, the Royal Naval Submarine School, is built inside the old Fort Blockhouse, one of the Solent Forts that are scattered around the area. The accommodation was good, with only four men to a cabin, and the food was better than most naval establishments. After work finished at four in the afternoon, the whole place appeared to switch off. It was a lot more relaxed than the basic training schools I had been used to and I actually began to enjoy my time there. My interest, initially somewhat lacking, began to increase and, as time went on I began to congratulate myself on swapping drafts with Paddy. Of course, the extra one pound and forty-four pence per day had nothing to do with it.

Even the duties at Dolphin seemed to be more enjoyable. There were only two real sentry points which were manned by trainees, the pier head and the quartermaster's booth. The pier head was the favourite, sitting in a small brick building watching the ships come and go in Portsmouth Harbour. The occasional naval tender would pull alongside, bringing men back from the Portsmouth pubs, but, apart from checking the security passes of those disembarking, there wasn't much to be done. If I were really lucky I would get the morning watch, from four till eight in the morning. Now, I know that sounds a little perverse, looking forward to getting up at that time of the day but, in the block of flats opposite, at seven each morning, a very nubile young lady used to arise from her slumbers. I'm not sure whether she was unaware of the power of Zeiss binoculars or just an exhibitionist, but her naked body walking around the living room and kitchen certainly helped many a young trainee submariner to rise early!

The quartermaster duty was only slightly more taxing. That was carried out in a small brick hut attached to the administration building, Alecto Colonnade, or, the Electric Lemonade as it was generally known. The quartermaster's tasks consisted mainly of making broadcasts on the tannoy system, announcing the high points of the establishment's daily routine. At night, the only task was to answer the phone.

At three o' clock one morning, I was in the quartermaster's hut, reading a three month old copy of the Navy News, when a strange bleating noise began to distract me. I looked around but could see nothing out of place and went back to the paper. The distraction continued and I found myself unable to concentrate. A detailed search of the six-foot by six-foot hut revealed a small box, just above head level. The bleating appeared to be coming from it and I climbed on the stool to take a closer look. A small light was flashing red. My curiosity deepened and I looked at the small metal plate on the side of the box. 'National Nuclear Warning System', it said. I could feel the blood draining out of my face. I remembered the Civil Defence training films we had been shown of nuclear attack precautions. How long was it we had? I seemed to remember the phrase 'Four minute warning'. Shit, it must have been going for three minutes already. I was just about to have my person cooked like a Chinese stir-fry and I didn't have a clue what to do. The films had gone on about putting tables against walls and covering them in earth before climbing under them to kiss your arse goodbye. Not too many tables or ready use soil patches here. Frantically I flicked through the pages of the Quartermaster's Emergency Procedures Manual. There was nothing in there to help. I picked up the internal phone and rang the duty officer's cabin. No reply. Oh good! No doubt he was interfering with the voluptuous body of some Wren Officer in her cabin. Well, if he thought he was just about to come, he was very much mistaken; he was just about to go. I almost laughed as I imagined an atomic mushroom ascending over Gosport and a blonde, petite Wren Officer looking into his eyes saying, "Oh Rupert, I felt the earth move," just before her lover's hairy arse burst into flames above her. This wasn't helping, three and a half minutes. I hope I died in the blast because I wasn't going to take the blame for this one. I aimed one rank higher and phoned the duty lieutenant commander. After three rings the phone was answered and a sleepy voice said, "Duty lieutenant commander."

Oh, thank God.

"Sir, it's the quartermaster, the National Nuclear warning has just gone off."

There was the slightest of pauses.

"Thank you quartermaster, keep me posted." There was a click as the phone went dead.

I stood there looking at the phone in disbelief. Keep him bloody posted. In fifteen seconds he wouldn't need to be kept bloody posted. We'd be dead. As if it would really matter, I thought to myself. At least I could blame him now, it won't be all my fault. I replaced the telephone handset in the cradle and sat down on the stool. What the hell was I to do now? The phone rang. I snatched it up.

"What did you say?"

I repeated my earlier message.

"How long has it been going?"

I looked at my watch, the four minute warning had now been sounding for five minutes. Perhaps some sharp eyed radar operator had spotted the attack early.

"Five minutes sir."

There was a pregnant pause. "Is there a telephone number on the alarm box?"

I climbed onto the stool and looked at the box. Oh, thank the Lord. "Yes sir."

I rang the number. Engaged? How can it be bloody engaged? We're all about to die horribly and the phone is engaged. I tried again, still engaged. I heard the door open and turned to see the duty lieutenant commander standing in the doorway. He was wearing his uniform jacket and cap over a very fetching pair of blue and white striped pyjamas.

I tried for an hour to get through. After ten minutes the officer was bored and retired to his bed to die. It wasn't until the following day that we found out what had happened. A new cleaner at the warning centre had found all the little buttons and knobs just a little too tempting. He had decided to find out what they did and had sent the entire nation into mass panic. Military forces all over the UK were sent to the highest state of readiness and prepared for all out nuclear war. I assume that the cleaner did not retain his post long enough to collect his Civil Service Pension. Nothing was ever said to me about it. Still, at least I was alive and still claiming my one pound forty-four pence a day submarine pay.

CHAPTER SEVEN

Following my basic submarine course I was introduced to the mysteries of the Valiant Class submarine. I became increasingly convinced, as time went on, that I had done the right thing when I had swapped with Paddy. It had been decided that, on joining the submarine, I would be working as a torpedo-man. I was trained in the types of weapons used onboard and their handling and firing systems. It had become fun to learn and I began to become impatient to get to sea.

The training of submariners is in three sections. The basic submarine course I had completed is Part 1, the course relating to the class of submarine in which a man will serve is Part 2 and, on reaching his submarine, the training begins for real.

My courses complete, I made the long journey north to Faslane Submarine Base. The home of the third and tenth submarine squadrons, it is located on the Gareloch, just outside Helensburgh, about 30 miles north west of Glasgow. I arrived and carried out the, by now, ritual joining routine. Unlike men serving in surface ships, submariners do not live aboard when alongside. The cramped conditions make it impractical to live on a submarine when it is not absolutely necessary, and there is insufficient storage space to allow personal possessions to be kept onboard. When alongside, at its home base or other naval port, the crew live in the naval barracks. In the home port a mess space ashore is kept for each man, and his kit, except for those few items required for sea, are kept there while he is away. The advantage of this is that, when a submarine is visiting a foreign port, or a UK port without a naval base, hotels are provided or a subsistence allowance is paid to each man. It is normal for subsistence to be paid in the UK, and for each man to find his own accommodation. Abroad, hotel rooms are booked in advance and these are on a bed and breakfast basis, paid for by the Navy. A small allowance is then paid, in cash advance, to each man, to allow him to purchase food ashore. This is a sore point with those serving on surface ships as, when abroad, they are required to spend their own money on beer, whereas submariners use their food allowance to finance their liquid diet.

Although I was now a member of the crew of HMS/M Courageous, I had not yet set foot on the boat. I slept my first night in HMS Neptune, the administration base serving the submarine squadrons at Faslane. The mess decks were very quiet and I soon fell asleep after my long journey. I was rudely awoken by the sounds of drunken men singing and shouting as the crew returned from their evening in the town. I kept my head down. I could not however ignore the keenly contested competition held in my mess to see who could light a fart and obtain the longest jet of flame. I lay in my bed mesmerised by the sight of grown men, laying on beds, legs akimbo, carrying out contortionist acts to get the lighter flame close to their arse. The competition was brought to a premature and noisy end when, what I later found out was a leading seaman, set fire to the hairs around his sphincter and left the room in a hurry to dunk his blistered backside in a sink of cold water. Discretion being the better part of valour, I decided that I would introduce myself when they were sober and not setting fire to sensitive areas of their anatomy.

The following morning, after a shower, I made my way to breakfast in the dining hall, several hundred yards from the accommodation blocks. It was bitterly cold and pouring with rain, the normal weather for Faslane throughout the majority of the year, as I was to discover during my numerous years there.

I walked from the dining room to the tunnel, which led from the base to the submarine jetties. Ministry of Defence Police were at the end of the tunnel controlling access. Only those with the proper passes were allowed entry and, even as a submariner, I was not allowed onto to the jetty where the Polaris missile submarines were berthed.

Several boats of various types were tied alongside and I slowly walked along, marvelling at the sleek look of them. All submarines are painted black and it may be this that gives them a sinister air. They appeared to be quite small, but, like an iceberg, about eighty percent of a submarine is always beneath the surface. I finally caught my first glimpse of Courageous. She was tied up alongside another submarine, across which I had to walk to get to her. The hatch was covered by a fibreglass hut, in which a sentry sat. I introduced myself and, amazingly, received a friendly smile and a guide was called to show me below. I was taken to the coxswain's office where I was actually made to feel welcome. Within a few minutes I had been directed to the fore-ends, also known as the torpedo compartment. On a Valiant class submarine, the torpedo room is on two levels. In the lower level are the torpedo tubes, six in all, two high and three across. Here are stowed all the torpedoes and mines that a submarine will carry to sea. In the upper level, on racks, which would, during time of war, carry extra torpedoes, are bunks for up to twenty four men. This is where I, as a Part Three trainee, would be sleeping, for the foreseeable future. It was, as I was soon to find out, a good place to sleep. It was more spacious, better ventilated and certainly less smelly, than the bunk space in which the majority of the crew slept. Privacy is almost non-existent in a submarine, and Courageous' sleeping arrangements would allow me precious little of it in my years aboard.

My first day was a haze. It was a mass of new faces and routines. I was introduced to virtually the whole crew, all of who seemed welcoming and eager to help me settle in. I was told about the daily routine and I was given an idea of the ship's programme for the coming months, which, luckily, involved a good deal of time at sea, and some visits to both UK and foreign ports. The one thing that was the same as my first day on Ark Royal was, yes, I was duty. I actually looked forward to sleeping on a submarine for the first time. As a trainee, the only duty I could carry out was casing sentry and I was to spend at least part of the night in the fibreglass hut above the hatch. Even that was fairly civilised. A heater had been fitted and a stool provided, it was fairly comfortable and I was only required to move outside once an hour. I was shown how to check the draught marks. These indicated how much of the boat was actually under water and thus, the crew could tell if it was slowly sinking. I was allocated the first (8pm to midnight) and morning (4am to 8am) watches. This was easy, I could even sleep from midnight to four and, so I was told, the whole duty watch were given a make and mend (afternoon off) the following day. The first watch was uneventful and, excited but tired, I turned in. No sheets and pillowcases here. Everyone was issued with a green naval issue sleeping bag. It was the only bedding issued for as long as the boat was at sea. There were no facilities which would allow anything bigger than a shirt to be washed and sleeping bags made of nylon do tend to become very smelly very quickly. Shortly before four am I was woken from my slumbers. This was incredible. On the Ark Royal it had been a bash on the side of the head by an anonymous fist. Here, I was brought a cup of strong, hot coffee by the person I was to relieve. I could see this was going to be a doddle.

I made my way to the casing, which was lashed by rain blowing down the loch from the north. The water around the boat was slapping against the sides and I could feel Courageous move, tugging at her ropes and bumping the wooden pontoon placed to protect her hull from damage by the submarine alongside. I huddled into my waterproofs and pulled the hood up over my head. The heater's warmth now seemed a little feeble and I was cold. Leaving the hut to read the draught marks was a chore. It was cold and wet and, walking on the narrow, sloping and slippery casing was dangerous. On more than one occasion I very nearly fell between the two submarines.

I had been on deck for two hours when a face appeared at the hatch.

"Go on then mate. You can go below now. Have a cuppa and warm up before breakfast".

I looked to see Dave Harwood, known to all onboard as 'Judy', one of my fellow torpedomen.

"Thanks," I replied, "but I thought I was here till eight."

"You've got to get ready for breakfast Chas."

How nice these submariners were. Two hours till breakfast and, already, I was being allowed to go below and warm up before sitting down to a good hot full English. "Thanks Judy." I said, with a smile.

"I'll have my bacon crispy." Said Judy with a smile, "And me egg runny."

I looked at him baffled. "What are you telling me for?" I asked.

He looked at me. "They haven't told you have they?"

"Told me what?"

"You are the morning watch trot sentry, therefore, you have to cook breakfast for the crew."

I looked at him, gob-smacked. Me, cook. He had to be joking; just because my name was Cooke it did not make me the Galloping Gourmet. I went below to the galley. It was about the size of the average household bathroom and about as well suited to cooking for a crew of submariners who would rip my face off if I didn't supply them with breakfast. I looked around. There were two small ovens, one electric hotplate and a deep fat fryer. There were all the ingredients, placed neatly on the steel work surface.

I have never sweated so much in my life. The bacon was, well, let us say crispy shall we. The fried eggs were about the consistency of a dog's rubber ball and the fried bread became shrapnel as it was attacked by knife and fork. The baked beans were warm and the sausages were cooked but cold. The professional ability of the cooks aboard Courageous was called into question when crewmembers began to congratulate me on my culinary skills. It appeared that I had got away with that one but, as I was to find out, there were plenty more little traps awaiting my clumsy attentions.

CHAPTER EIGHT

"Diving now, diving now."

The ship's tannoy system crackled into life. A hiss came from the main vent, close to where I was sitting, and a faint whoosh could be heard as the air left the main ballast tanks, to be replaced by seawater rushing in and making the boat negatively buoyant. My image of men rushing to the front of the submarine as it hurtled below the water in a matter of seconds was dashed. That sort of thing just doesn't happen to a nuclear submarine. It can take four or five minutes for the boat to disappear beneath the waves and it is a slow, almost laboured event. A slight tilt of the deck as the bow slowly began to dip beneath the waves was all that could be felt. No squealing of steel plates and popping of rivets under pressure, no panic stricken dash of men to their stations to prepare for depth charges. If I hadn't been able to see the depth gauge between the dials of the torpedo firing gear control panel, I wouldn't have known that we had descended to sixty feet. No pressure on the eardrums and no rush of water past the hull. The slight roll that the boat had experienced on the surface had gone and, against what I had expected, it was quiet and still. Courageous was moving along at eight knots, pushing the water aside without even a ripple on a surface marked only by the white feather of wake caused by the periscope. The overall impression the crew gave was one of professional boredom. My heart was pounding: At last, I was at sea on a submarine in its element, beneath the waves and unseen by those above. And, what was more, we were on our way to Gibraltar. I didn't know it at the time but this was to be one of my many visits to The Rock. Over the years, unlike many sailors, I actually came to love the place. Its quaint Englishness with a Spanish come Moorish air just seemed to strike a chord with me. Little was I to know what fun and trouble I would have there over the years but, for now, all I wanted to do was get to know my job onboard, get to know the rest of my crewmates and get to Gibraltar for my first submariner's run ashore. I was just eighteen and, oh boy, was I going to make good use of the fact that I could now legally drink!

We had been at sea for three days and, as I walked along the narrow passageway, past the junior and senior rate's mess decks I heard a hiss. Was this escaping air? Perhaps a hydraulic leak. Maybe there was water pouring in through a hole in the pressure hull and I was destined to drown before my first ran ashore with my new found crewmates. There it was again, pssst. I looked around and saw the Coxswain, the First Lieutenant and several rather hefty sailors, hiding in the 2nd Coxswain's store. I looked at the Coxswain and realised that he had been making the noise. Once again he psssted at me, and beckoned to me in a conspiratorial manner. As I walked toward him he held a finger to his lips. I approached the door of the tiny storage area and was immediately dragged inside. Oh God, male rape, flashed through my mind. I began to struggle.

"For Christ's sake shut up Chas, he'll hear us." Said the Coxswain.

I began to think that this was, perhaps, some maniacal game of hide and seek. But who was looking for us and how many did he have to count up to before he came searching.

The inside of the store was in virtual darkness, the only light coming from the poorly fitting frame around the door. Someone shone a torch in my face and, like all torches onboard, it had a red filter across the lens to permit only a slight glow. This was to prevent the night vision of the officer manning the periscope from being ruined in the event that a torch was needed to illuminate something in the pitch black of the control room at night.

I could just make out that the torch was being held by the First Lieutenant, the second in command of the submarine.

"Now, Cooke, I have a job for you." He said. "It's that time of year when we must all gird our loins and put our collective brawn into the fray and ensure that nobody gets hurt".

What was he on about? Had he gone mad? Was this some bizarre and perverted submariner's ritual?

The Coxswain came to his aid. "Chas, it's time for Ben's inoculations."

The light dawned. Ben Naylor was the Torpedo Instructor. He had joined the submarine service in 1953, four years before I was born. He was a red haired version of Bluto from the Popeye cartoons. He had muscles where no person had any right to have muscles. From his bushy red beard to his shovel sized hands he just oozed power and strength. I had been given a graphic demonstration of his strength only a few days before. Whilst loading a one and a half ton of torpedo into a tube, the tail had stuck on a ridge in the steel rails on which it was carried into the tube. Nothing would budge it and the tube inner door was open with the torpedo half in and half out, a dangerous state for any submarine. Ben got a huge iron bar and, placing one end of the bar on the offending beam, passing the bar under the tail of the torpedo, he put his shoulder under the other end of the bar. With a slight grunt he lifted the back of the torpedo fully three inches clear of the obstruction. He'd hardly broken sweat. But Ben had one weakness, his Achilles heel. He was petrified of needles and injections. During the annual round of inocculations on the submarine, Ben was conspicuous by his absence. During the previous attempt to give him the various jabs required by men of the Royal Navy, three of the crew had required stitches and one a plaster cast. That goes without mentioning the various bruised testicles, eyes and all points in between.

The Coxswain revealed his plan. It required a sacrificial lamb. I wonder who that was going to be. I looked around. Well, it wasn't going to be the First Lieutenant. It was the Coxswain's plan so it wasn't going to be him. Eventually, without the use of too much brainpower, I realised that I was it.

In the passageway, immediately outside the door to the torpedo compartment is a ladder. It goes to two small office spaces on the deck above. The ladder formed an integral part of the plan and was to be the only protection I would have from the wrath of Naylor. Either side of the ladder were two further small spaces with doors, one we were in, sweating away in conspiratorial stupidity, and the other was the Coxswain's office. I was quietly ushered out of the door of the storeroom with a packet of Ben's favourite pipe tobacco in my hand. I looked to my right and left, the biggest men on the boat were crammed into the two spaces on either side of the ladder, peeking through the crack between door and frame.

"Get on with it you knob." Came the encouraging voice of the Coxswain.

I cleared my throat and called to Ben who was sitting on the step just inside the door to the torpedo compartment doing paperwork.

"Excuse me TI, the Coxswain asked me to give you this." I said in what I hoped was a normal voice.

"What's that then?" asked Ben.

"Your month's ration of duty free pipe tobacco TI." I said.

I could feel the sweat trickling down my back and a small bead was making its way down my face, irritating and making me twitch.

"Well bring it in and give it here then."

"I can't."

"Why the hell not?"

Oh shit, he'd got me. God he was a clever bastard. Why couldn't I go to him? Why should he, a Chief Petty Officer have to come to me, a sprog? Suddenly it came to me. At the time I thought it was brilliant. Now, I can't believe he actually fell for it.

"I trod in some dog shit and I don't want to tread it all over the torpedo compartment."

There was an audible groan from the Coxswain and a snigger or two from the other men hidden in the cramped spaces either side.

Ben got up and moved toward me. I took a small step back and held the tobacco close to the ladder and between two rungs. Ben reached for it and I moved back slightly. A puzzled look came over his face and he reached forward, through the rungs of the ladder.

There was an eruption of hairy arsed sailors bursting from all corners. Three of them got behind Ben and pushed him hard against the ladder. The remainder grabbed a section of his huge, hairy, tattoo covered, arm and pulled it through the ladder rungs. He was held fast. I saw a puzzled look come across his face. It didn't last long. The Coxswain appeared with a hypodermic syringe in his hand and all hell broke loose. There were men flying in all directions, the sound of bone upon flesh rang through the air. I even saw the First Lieutenant dumped, unceremoniously, onto his backside due to a collision with a flying sailor. The needle was rammed into Ben's upper arm and the contents ejected into his blood stream.

Ben's final words before he fainted were "Cooke, I'm going to rip...."

There were men running away all around me. Nobody wanted to be there when Ben came round. It was alright for them, I had to work for the bloke. I was going to die, there was no other possible end to this tale of woe and deceipt. Shaking and sweating profusely I hid in the junior rate's mess drinking tea and smoking endless cigarettes.

Ben never mentioned the event. It was as though it had never happened. Speaking to him some years later, just before he retired, I found that Ben was deeply ashamed of his, as he saw it, unreasonable fear. Once it had happened he would never mention it again. Mind you, I still wonder how a man of Ben's size can hide for two weeks, in the confines of a submarine, before being found. He managed it the next year.

CHAPTER NINE

The trip was over almost before it began. The slight bump, as the submarine finally touched the jetty, was the sign I had been waiting for. Many of the crew had been to Gibraltar before, but not me. I could hardly wait to see this fortress dependency. It was famous as a naval base and the guardian of the entrance to the Mediterranean Sea. The order to fall out from harbour stations was given and there was a general rush toward the mess decks and bunk spaces where holdalls, containing those precious civilian clothes were stored. I walked from the torpedo compartment along the passageway, past the mess. Up the ladder to the control room and it was only a short walk to the main access hatch and my first glimpse of Gibraltar.

I poked my head out of the hatch into bright sunlight and a deep blue sky. Not a cloud to be seen. As I stepped onto the casing the panorama that is Gibraltar was before me. The Rock of Gibraltar, and what a rock. The steep sided limestone cliffs rose above the small town at its foot. There was very little room for the town or the people of Gibraltar to settle at its base. I was later to find out that there are more miles of road inside the rock itself than outside.

The sun was pleasantly warm without being overpowering and there was a cool breeze coming from the sea. The harbour was packed with both Royal and Merchant Naval vessels of all shapes and sizes. The sea was the wonderful dark blue for which the Mediterranean is famous.

"Get out the way you wanker."

Back to reality with a jolt then. By standing in the middle of the narrow casing I had blocked the access to the gangway for those who were already disappearing ashore, mainly those who had visited Gibraltar before and were eager to visit their good friends, the bar staff of the local hostelries.

There are several differences between a visit abroad by a submarine and a visit abroad by a destroyer, frigate or other surface ship, or skimmer, as they were known to all submariners. The first difference is that, as a submariner, I earned one pound and forty-four pence per day extra, thus I could buy more beer. Secondly, a man working on a surface ship would be expected to work during the day, even when visiting a foreign port, and would only be allowed ashore out of working hours. I, on the other hand, as a submariner, would not be expected to return to the submarine until the day it sailed, unless I was required as a member of the duty watch for a night during the visit, thus, I could drink more beer. A man on a surface ship would have to return to that ship to sleep each night and was subject to scrutiny by the regulating staff at the gangway and could be arrested if drunk. I, as a submariner, was accommodated in a hotel, paid for by the Royal Navy, breakfast included, and therefore I was not subject to scrutiny by anyone, thus, I could drink more beer. Finally, men on surface ships were provided, onboard, with their three meals a day. Submariners were not, and, to make up for this cruelly unfair state of nourishment, the Royal Navy gave me, in cash, an allowance each day to purchase lunch and dinner. Therefore I had loads of money, who eats when abroad anyway, thus, I could buy more beer.

I fought my way back down the ladder against the oncoming tide of submariners who could smell the alcohol and hear the women calling their names. I collected my holdall from the torpedo compartment and made my way back to the casing and onto the jetty. A coach had been provided to take us to our hotels. The officers were accommodated in the 5 star Rock Hotel, the senior rates in the 4 star Queen's Hotel and the junior rates, well away from the others, in the 3 star Caleta Palace Hotel.

I was amazed by the number of cars on the limited number of roads in Gibraltar. It couldn't take much more than twenty minutes to walk from one side of the rock to the other and yet, the place was full of big Mercedes saloons, all travelling at not much more than walking pace.

My first glimpses of Gibraltar itself, Main Street, the airport and the cable car to the summit of the rock itself.

The bus pulled into the sweep in front of the Caleta Palace Hotel, right on one of the few beaches on Gibraltar at Catlan Bay. I managed to grab my key and dashed upstairs to my room. I wanted to have a shower, get changed and have a look around Gib. Oh, and buy some of that beer of course. I went into my room and was confronted by George, the steward with whom I was sharing. He was naked and standing next to the open window, overlooking the swimming pool and beach, with a can of beer in his hand. The window was full-length, floor to ceiling. The swimming pool, with a corrugated perspex roof over it, to protect bathers from the sun, was directly below and the view across Catlan Bay was superb. George was in full view of the other hotel guests lounging at the poolside. Now George was not, and would never be, a bronzed Adonis type. He was about five feet four inches standing up and five feet six inches laying down. His voluminous belly told many a tale of nights spent in bars quaffing pint after pint of cheap ale. He was already pissed as a fart.

"Alright George?" I asked.

"Hello Chas me old mate." He replied.

He had eyes like a pools coupon, one at home and one away. I wondered how anyone could be that drunk so soon after arriving, after all, he hadn't even been into town yet. I looked around the room and there, beside his bed, was his holdall. It contained what appeared to be one pair of jeans, one T shirt, a couple of pairs of underpants and a rather large number of cans of beer, half of which were, by now, empty and were scattered across the floor by his bed.

He grinned at me with that 'I've either had a severe stroke or I'm completely bladdered' kind of lopsided smile.

"I think I'll go for a swim." He stated.

He made his way unsteadily across the room to his bag and, delving beneath the beer cans, produced the skimpiest pair of crimson swimming trunks I had ever seen. He fell onto the bed giggling as he put both legs through the same leg hole. Eventually, with a frown of deep concentration, he managed to extricate himself from the tangled shred of nylon and pulled them up around his waist. His beer gut was hanging over the front of the trunks and, at the rear, they were so tight that they had disappeared up the crack of his arse leaving his bare, and not inconsiderable buttocks, open to full view. He selected another can of beer from his bag, inspecting it carefully to make sure that it was up to the required standard for such a connoisseur of the hop liqueur.

"George, you can't walk through the hotel dressed like that." I said.

He looked at me thoughtfully.

"You're absolutely right Chas," he said, "I don't want to upset the guests do I?" And with that, clutching the can of beer, he walked across to the window and, unsteadily, climbed onto the low windowsill.

"George, for Christ's sake, what are you doing?"

Without a backward glance George flung himself from the window and hurtled toward the ground, three floors below. I heard an enormous crash and screams echoed from the poolside beneath. I ran across to the window and looked out, expecting to see George, dead, on the ground some thirty-five feet below.

As I peered out of the window I saw, instead, a George shaped hole in the perspex roof of the swimming pool. Half of the water had left the pool as George had entered and many of the sunbathers at the poolside were shaking themselves, like saturated spaniels. George was calmly treading water in the centre of the pool, directly beneath the hole in the roof. His head was bleeding, leaving a pink trail in the water. He looked up, waved to me, took a sip from the can of beer still clutched firmly in his hand and called.

"Chas old boy, the water's lovely, you really should come on in."

There was general pandemonium as several white shirted and bow tied staff ran to the pool. George was unceremoniously dragged from the water and hauled away, bowing to the crowd as he went. The Naval Provost was called and I last saw George being placed into the rear of a naval minibus and thence, off to H.M.S. Rook, the naval shore establishment, where he was placed into the cells, to await collection by the duty officer from the submarine. George's run ashore in Gibraltar had lasted the grand total of fifty seven minutes, a record for George from what I later came to know of him. I had the room to myself for the remainder of that visit to Gibraltar.

Gibraltar is often thought of as an island. It is, in fact connected to the Spanish mainland but, at that time, the continuing argument between the Spanish and British governments, over the sovereignty of the state, was raging on. This had resulted in the border between the two being shut. The only way to travel to Spain was to catch the ferry across to Tangier and then another ferry back to Spain. This meant that Gibraltar was isolated. The town of Gibraltar itself, and that is all there is, can only be about the size of a large English village. It has one main shopping street, funnily enough known as Main Street, in which the majority of the shops and bars are situated. Any sailor in Gibraltar had only to walk along Main Street and look through the windows of the many bars and pubs to find his crew mates.

The shops were a mass of colour and bartering was the accepted method of deciding upon a price for any item that was for sale. I loved the place. Everyone spoke English, the locals seemed genuinely glad to see us and English sterling was the currency, so you knew if someone was trying to rip you off in the shops and bars, not that it often happened.

Main Street was packed with people as I walked along it. The pubs and bars were doing a roaring trade, mainly from the sailors ashore from the numerous ships in the harbour. Unlike many towns where the majority of the people in the street are drunk, there was never any feeling of being threatened. The sun seemed to bring out the best in people and everyone was happily drunk rather than fighting drunk.

I came across the rest of the crew in The Horseshoe, a very British style pub in the centre of Main Street. They were doing their best to drink Gibraltar dry. I was summoned to the group and immediately a pint was placed in front of me. The tone had been set and the drinking continued into the afternoon and through to the early evening. I began to feel lightheaded and, after several hours, I was glad when there was a general move away from the bar and out into the street.

"Where are we going, Topsy?" I asked a large stoker.

"It's time for a rabbit run." He said.

I hadn't got a clue what he was on about but, I suppose I might as well go along with it. I was soon to find out that a rabbit run is submariner slang for souvenir shopping.

I tagged along with Topsy and a couple of other lads from the boat and we must have gone into every shop in Main Street. Nobody seemed to be buying anything though.

"There's one." Topsy exclaimed.

He was standing, unsteadily, in front of a shop window, pointing. There, in the middle of the display, was a huge fibre optic lamp. It was just what Topsy wanted, or rather, it was just what Topsy's wife wanted. Apparently he was under strict orders to buy one whilst in Gibraltar where they could be purchased for a much lower price than they were demanding in Britain.

We entered the shop and Topsy took up a gladiatorial stance. He was ready to barter and he was going to get a deal out of this shopkeeper, if it was the last thing he did. The beer had given Topsy Dutch courage and he thrust out his chest and demanded to know the price of the object of his wife's desires.

"Twenty one pounds" said the Asian shopkeeper.

Topsy threw a glance over his shoulder. He raised his eyebrows in that 'I don't think so' kind of way. This was where the serious bartering was about to begin.

"How much?"

"Twenty one pounds."

"Now come along, we must be able to do better than that."

My God he was good.

"Twenty one pounds is my final price."

Topsy threw another glance toward the group behind him. He grinned and cocked his head on one side.

"Now I think we can change your mind here," he said to the shopkeeper, "I'll give you twenty two."

There was a fit of laughter from one of the group and Topsy whipped round with his fingers to his lips.

"Shut up. You'll ruin me chances if you piss him off by laughing at him." He hissed at the guilty party.

He turned back to the shopkeeper.

"Look, I'll tell you what I'll do," he said, "I'll give you twenty three, and that's my final offer."

"Twenty four." Came the reply from the shopkeeper.

I was trying so hard not to laugh that my stomach was hurting. Several other members of our group had made their way to the door and were desperately trying not to burst out laughing.

"Now, I'm not an unfair man, but I will not be fobbed off," said Topsy, "I can go to twenty five, and no more."

"Twenty six."

The tears were rolling down my face. One of the stokers was laughing so much that he lost control of his bladder and a dark, slowly spreading stain appeared across the front of his jeans.

Topsy took a deep breath, threw back his shoulders and continued to barter. "Twenty seven and not a penny more."

"Twenty eight."

Topsy took his wallet from his pocket and counted the notes inside. He delved into his pockets and took out a handful of loose change. He turned to the group who, by now, were helpless with mirth.

"Can someone lend me some dosh till we get back to the hotel?" He asked.

It was worth a few quid to see a spectacle like this. We all searched through the coins in our pockets and handed over a few more pounds. Topsy laid it out on the counter of the shop and meticulously counted it.

"I have here, with the help of my good friends, a grand total of twenty nine pounds and eighty three pence, it is all I have and I will not be moved on that price."

The shopkeeper made his final push.

"If you can make it thirty pounds I will reluctantly sell it to you, but I am losing money on the deal."

Topsy looked again through his pockets. He managed to find a few more coppers and he turned to the group once again for help. One of the lads handed over the difference. Topsy turned and placed the money on the counter. He carefully counted out the notes and then the coins, placing the cash in neat and tidy piles on the cluttered counter. He insisted that the shopkeeper also count it with him, a process that took some considerable time. Topsy wanted to make sure that the shopkeeper knew who had won this round.

Eventually the thirty pounds was handed over and the trophy transferred to Topsy's custodianship. He turned to the group with a grin,

"Yeeeessss." He shouted, punching the air in victorious celebration.

The group erupted into fits of uncontrollable laughter, the shopkeeper rubbed his hands and Topsy strolled from the shop his head held high and his trophy under his arm.

We retired to another bar for a celebratory drink. We had to buy Topsy's beer for him, he had spent all his money in the shop. Talking to other members of the group I learned that this was a regular performance after Topsy had had a few beers. He never could get the hang of bartering but he thought he was brilliant at it. He could not understand why people found it so difficult.

"It's rude not to barter. It's a local custom and one must respect local culture." He explained to the group.

After several hours I decided that enough was enough. My beer level had reached full and I was becoming tired and confused. I made my way back to the hotel where I fell into a deep sleep for the night.

The following morning I woke just in time for breakfast. I went downstairs to the dining room where many of the crew were still sitting around tables sipping coffee and clutching their throbbing heads. I hoped I looked a bit better than most of them did, because I felt like death warmed up. I saw Topsy's group sitting at a table in the comer and joined them. I ordered a strong coffee and some toast. I noticed that Topsy was looking particularly ill.

"You alright Topsy?" I asked.

"She's going to bleedin' kill me." He said, looking around the group through bloodshot eyes. "I'm right in the cack now."

"What's the matter then?" I asked, concerned.

"I only left me fibre optic lamp in the pub last night."

There was uproar as several members of the group fell off their chairs laughing. My head was throbbing, and laughing that much isn't good for you when you have a hang over. Topsy just sat there, his head in his hands.

"I really bartered hard for that."

I had to leave the table.

CHAPTER TEN

My run ashore in Gibraltar was almost complete, but not quite. There was still the matter of the courtesy side of the visit. Naval ships abroad are there to represent the Royal Navy and Great Britain. Gibraltar is mostly very British anyway so there were very few official functions in which the crew was expected to take part. There was one duty to perform however, the football match against H.M.S. Rook.

Now, our submarine had a crew of 110, of who about twelve percent had any aspirations toward athletic prowess of any kind. On the other side of the balance, H.M.S. Rook was a large shore establishment, which was bursting at the seams with suntanned sailors who had little else to do but keep fit and excel at any kind of sport. At the time of our visit Rook supplied no less than six members of the Royal Navy Football Team. They were a superbly trained and coordinated eleven who had not lost a match in over two years. We were a bunch of drunken, hung over salad dodgers who would go to the ends of the earth to avoid physical exertion of any kind. We did however have one or two men who were under the vast misapprehension that they had only to give the nod to be selected for the national team. In reality, they had all the coordination and ball control of a three-toed sloth with rickets. The other problem with the forthcoming fixture was that Gibraltar has only one grass football pitch, and that is the national stadium. We, surprisingly, were not allowed to play on its hallowed turf. We were booked on one of the two cinder and gravel pitches across the road from H.M.S. Rook's main entrance. The kick off was scheduled for two in the afternoon, a gross error of judgement on the part of our Captain who had arranged the fixture. The bars and pubs in Gibraltar had, by that time, been open for four hours.

Because of the playing surface nobody would even consider playing in goal. I, as the youngest and newest member of the crew, who had, under a cloud of utter stupidity, hinted that I was a better than average goalkeeper, had been nominated to play between the sticks. At five to two most of our team had made their way, in varying stages of intoxication, to the pitch. We looked fairly bedraggled, dressed as we were in an assortment of civvies, ranging from jeans and T-shirt to shorts and flip-flops. Only about half of those assembled had any suitable form of footwear, the rest deciding that, to give us some chance, they would play in steaming boots, the ankle high, steel toe capped boots worn at sea. In contrast, across the other side of the pitch, were fourteen immaculately turned out sporting gods. They were dressed in matching white tracksuits with red and blue trim. The back was emblazoned with the words 'H.M. S. ROOK—NAVY CUP WINNERS—1970/l/2/3'. They were deep in a tactical huddle, their manager directing the team like a well practiced orchestra. We finished off our cans of beer and bottles of vino as we changed. Someone had borrowed a football kit before we left Faslane. It was yellow shirts, red shorts and an assortment of odd socks. The shirts were various shades of yellow and had more holes than material. It was obvious that they had never meant to be worn by grown men. The shirts barely reached the shorts and, in some cases there remained a large expanse of flaccid belly exposed to the elements. The shorts were so tight they were almost pornographic. More like a G-string than shorts in some cases.

The opposition stripped off their tracksuits to expose immaculate white shirts with red and blue trim, navy blue shorts with white and red trim and black socks with red white and blue trim at the top. They all seemed to be wearing expensive football boots. We could smell the aroma of liniment across the width of the pitch. In contrast all I could smell on our side was the odour of stale beer, the occasional fart and, for God's sake, three of our blokes were smoking roll ups.

Across the pitch a complicated set of stretching and warm up exercises was under way. We had another beer. The touchline had started to fill up with Rook supporters come to watch the latest sacrifice take place. There was a group of men from our submarine, including the Captain, First Lieutenant and most of the officers. Standing slightly apart was the junior and senior rates who had managed to prise themselves away from the bar long enough to cheer us on, or take the piss, I wasn't sure which. Most of our supporters clutched alcohol in a variety of disguises. The Rook supporters actually had flags and banners. It looked as though they were serious about this. Even a few locals, starved of any real sporting contest in Gibraltar, had turned out to watch the action.

I took my place between the goalposts as the two teams formed up. Rook players were sprinting on the spot and warming up. Our lads were, for the most part sat on the ground while those near the touchline were taking this opportunity to scrounge a last drag on a fag or a swig from a bottle. Johnny Musto, who had been nominated as our captain for the match strolled to the centre circle. His steaming boots were slopping about on his feet as he couldn't be bothered to buy new laces and his shorts were cutting off the blood supply to his lower limbs. He kept trying to pluck the shorts from the cleft between his buttocks as he walked forward. The referee tossed a coin and the two captains watched it fall. Johnny immediately began to shout and swear. He pushed the opposing captain in the chest and took a drunken swing at the referee. Luckily he missed. I gathered we had lost the toss. Two of our team managed to pull Johnny away and Rook's captain placed the ball on the centre spot. The whistle blew and the ball was smartly and professionally passed forward a few inches before being delivered with pinpoint accuracy to the left-winger. Out of the comer of my eye I saw Big Bert Jameson, six feet three and nineteen stone of giant malevolence, hurtle across the pitch from our left wing. He launched into a huge sliding tackle and took out two of the Rook players. Bit harsh, I thought. After all, they hadn't even touched the ball as yet. He rose from the cloud of cinder dust and, as it cleared, there were two athletic young men lying on the ground clutching legs, ankles and testicles. Obviously Bert had followed through in the tackle and used a few illegal moves under the cover of the dust cloud. There was a stunned silence punctuated by the shrill blast of the ref's whistle. He called Bert across. I could see that the ref was a little upset. He sent Bert off. Great, nine seconds gone and we were down to ten men.

The free kick was taken and the ball was moved toward my goal area. Not to worry, my defence will see me okay. There was my left back, known to all as Billy Whizz, because of his ability to move slower than any other member of the crew. The forward with the ball gave a shimmy of the hips and Billy, confused and dazzled by his skill, and with his sense of balance sorely diminished by an excess of alcohol, fell flat on his arse and promptly vomited in his own lap. Oh well, just me between the forward and a certain goal. I moved toward him and he let fly with a ferocious right-footed shot. I flew through the air and a huge cheer erupted from our supporters as the ball sank into my scrotum and then rebounded before going behind for the corner.

"Oh, good save, Cooke, well done young man." Shouted the First Lieutenant.

"Oh, shit, right in the bollocks." Came a cry from the junior rate section of our fans. I dragged myself from the ground and modestly took the praise of the team as I tried to rub some feeling into my testicles.

"Come on Chas," said one of the team, "No time to masturbate, we're playing football here!"

I hobbled back to my goal, walking like John Wayne after a week on a horse, my eyes watering and my groin throbbing. The corner was taken and I flew from my goal in the general direction of the ball. Out of the corner of my eye I could see Johnny Musto firmly grasping the testicles of the opposition centre forward, who was doubled up in pain. I clenched my fist in preparation for the punch. Right on target. I heard the grunt as my knuckles connected with the side of the opponent's head. He went down like a sack of shit and the ball firmly flew past and out of play for a throw in. We had survived the first attack.

The throw was taken by a colour-blind idiot who threw it straight to their inside left, the Royal Navy's star player. He weaved and dribbled past three players and was clear on goal. Down to me again I suppose. As he sprinted toward the edge of my penalty area, the ball glued to the toe of his foot, I made my move. I sprinted toward him, screaming as loud as I could.

"Come on then you arsehole!"

He hesitated, but not for long. I don't think this tactic was in any book he had read. We continued toward each other, the closing speed was frightening. I threw myself sideways onto the ground and slid along the cinder and gravel, protected a little by my jeans tucked into my football socks. I took both of his legs and, almost in slow motion, he carried out two somersaults and even gained enough height to manage a half twist and a barrel roll. There was a sickening thud as he hit the ground. I grasped the ball, which had broken free. The ref obviously decided that it had been a fair challenge as I had emerged from the dust cloud with the ball in my hands.

During the break in play, while the naval ambulance arrived to cart the unfortunate soccer star off to the sick bay, I managed a quick fag and a can of beer. Several other members of the team also took the opportunity to refresh themselves. I could see their trainer complaining to our Captain of the tactics we were employing. His protest seemed to be falling on deaf ears and I heard the Captain tell him to "Piss off and stop whingeing."

The first half came to an end and we had managed to keep the score at nil, nil. There was a sense of incredulity amongst the opposition and their trainer was forcefully giving them new tactics for the second half.

They were sucking on oranges and encouraging each other to new heights. We had a beer each and several players disappeared over to the fence to relieve themselves.

A shrill blast on the ref's whistle brought the half time refreshments to a close. The two teams formed up and, even from the goalmouth, I could see that some of the enthusiasm had gone out of the opposition. We kicked off and the ball was passed to our centre half, Zip Newlyn. This was the longest spell of possession we had managed so far. The ball was belted up field and was taken neatly on the chest by the Rook right back. He moved forward and cut inside toward the centre circle. Eight of our nine remaining outfield players headed towards him leaving huge expanses of the field uncovered. I tried to direct the troops from the penalty area but they weren't listening. They had tasted blood and they wanted more. As they bore down upon him the right back did the most sensible thing he could: he got rid of the ball, passing it deftly to the right wing. Once again Billy Whizz was my only line of defence and once again a slight shimmy of the hips put him on his arse in the dust. He looked around in bewilderment as the winger moved past him toward my goal. I tried the, by now, familiar tactic of running at him screaming. He was smart this one. Just as I hurled myself to the ground with every intention of breaking both his legs he stopped in his tracks. I was stranded on the ground and had come up three yards short of him. He calmly placed his toe under the ball and scooped it over me. It bounced three times, before trickling into the net to a raucous round of cheering from his supporters. We were one nil down. Bollocks.

I was determined that I would repay the winger. He'd made me look stupid in front of my mates. I never had the chance. From the kick off the ball was booted as hard as possible at the opposition players. By some fluke it struck a knee and flew out of play for a corner. It was the only time we had managed to get close to their goal and everybody wanted a piece of this action. There were twenty players in the Rook penalty area. I was feeling very lonely in my empty half of the pitch. Tiny Tillman took the kick. The ball floated majestically across the goalmouth and there was a bloodcurdling scream. One of the Rook defenders leapt into the air and the ball cannoned off the back of his head and flew past the mesmerised goalkeeper. Bloody hell, we'd scored. One all. The crowd went mad. The Rook defender that had just scored the own goal went madder still. He flew out of the penalty box and ran straight toward Dave Harwood who was jogging innocently back to the half way line.

"You bastard." He screamed.

Dave turned round, the picture of innocence and looked at the referee pleadingly.

His own teammates grabbed the Rook defender and pulled him away. Dave jogged back toward me and stood next to me in the goalmouth.

"What was that all about Dave?" I asked.

"I think he objected to having this shoved up his arse." He replied, pulling a sailmaker's needle from the waistband of his shorts. It was a three-inch long stainless steel spike used for sewing heavy canvas.

"It went right in up to the hilt." He said with a grin and jogged away to join in the remainder of the match.

There were several bouts of artistic football by the Rook team, punctuated by an equal number of brutal fouls by us, which kept the score at one all for some considerable time. But they had found our weak spot; Billy Whizz. Again he was approached by an athletic sailor with a ball magically attached to his foot. Another quick swerving sidestep and, once again, Billy's arse hit the dust. Only a last minute, blatant trip, saved another certain goal.

They tried again, and once more Billy hit the floor with a puzzled expression. He was absolutely rat arsed and was just completely thrown by any rapid change of direction. His legs couldn't keep up with his brain.

For the fourth time the little winger ran toward Billy. I saw Billy's shoulders hunch and his head sink into his neck. There was a determination about him I had never seen before. Again the winger shimmied. Billy didn't move. He stood stock-still and swung both arms from behind his back at throat height. The momentum of the winger, going in the opposite direction, led him directly into the scimitar like sweep of Billy's muscular forearms and there was a split second where the winger's body had stopped but his feet continued to move. Both legs came up off the ground as he was struck square in the Adam's apple. There was an audible gasp from both sets of spectators. A loud cheer came from the contingent of local residents, which had now swelled in number. Obviously the word had got round that blood was on the cards. The winger hit the ground with a sickening thud landing flat on his back. Oh my lord, he's killed him, I thought. It didn't take long for that fear to be dispelled. Billy took half a pace back and then slammed the sole of his right boot into the groin of the prostrate winger.

"That'll teach you not to make me look a twat."

The whole crowd took a sharp intake of breath and, I noticed, several onlookers unconsciously grabbed their own testicles in sympathy. A high pitched scream erupted from the horizontal footballer and he doubled up like a long bow. Well, at least that proved he was alive.

A huge melee erupted as players from both sides pitched into the ensuing brawl. The referee went purple blowing his whistle to no avail and, in the end walked off of the pitch muttering that the match was abandoned. Oh well. At least we hadn't lost.

"Well played Courageous," came the lilting tones of the First Lieutenant's voice from the touch line, "very well played indeed chaps."

The team, swelled with pride in their majestic performance, retired to one of the many bars to celebrate. Beer was drunk in huge quantities and then, at about ten o'clock, we became aware of a rumpus outside. As one, pints in hand, the team walked out into Main Street. People were running in all directions. Several policemen were running, against the tide, in the opposite direction toward the end of the street.

We followed in the hope that something worth watching was taking place. It was. There on a fourth floor balcony of The Queen's Hotel, stood the Coxswain, the chief petty officer responsible for discipline on the submarine. He was naked from the waist down and was singing 'O Sole Mio' at the top of his voice, large whisky in hand, whilst urinating on the public passing beneath his balcony. It was a good job we were leaving in the morning. I don't think Gibraltar was quite ready for Courageous just yet.

CHAPTER ELEVEN

It was five in the morning as we struggled onto the coach, hangovers at the ready, for the short trip back to the dockyard. We were sailing in two hours. A large exercise was taking place in the Mediterranean and we were to play the part of a Russian submarine tasked with attacking the main fleet.

We slipped from the jetty at exactly seven a.m. and made our way slowly out of Gibraltar. As soon as we had sufficient water under the keel we dived and once more the crew settled back into the watch-keeping routine. We worked a two watch system, which meant that we worked twelve hours a day in two six hour sessions. I was in first watch and I worked from 1am to 7 am and then 1pm to 7pm. Seven days a week, that means an eighty four hour basic weeks work. On top of that, when needed at action stations or watch stand to, the whole crew would be working. During an exercise that could mean a twenty hour day, leaving only four hours in which to eat, sleep and drink. It was a punishing routine and, on return home after a long trip, many submariners found it extremely difficult to adapt to the normal hours that wives and girlfriends expected their men to adhere to. The divorce rate in the submarine service is the highest of any of the services and to be a submariners wife takes a special kind of woman.

While the husband is away at sea no contact with home is possible. Telephones don't work under the sea and there are no postboxes in the middle of the ocean. The wife is, in all respects, totally on her own whilst her husband is at sea. The navy tries to ease the burden by allowing 'familygrams' to be sent. The wife is given a sheet of paper for each week that her man is expected to be away. On the sheet are thirty squares and the wife is allowed to put a word in each square, with the first two being the name and rank of her husband. The completed form is sent to the submarine base where it is checked. If there is any mention of dates or locations, relating to the submarines deployment, the message is not sent. All being checked and in order, radio traffic permitting, the words are transmitted by radio to the submarine. This is received and written out longhand by the radio operator on the submarine who passes it on for the Communications Officer to check for any sign of bad news. If there is any the message is not given to the man concerned. If all is in order then the message is printed and placed on the ship's noticeboard for the man to collect. It is a source of real worry if an expected familygram does not turn up on time. I saw men almost frantic with worry because their message was a day or two later than expected. Of course, if the submarine was busy and the radios were engaged in sending and receiving signals, the familygrams would be delayed until a suitable gap in the radio schedule could be found. Luckily I was single and I received no familygrams whilst on Courageous, but they would come to play a big part in my life later on in my submarine service.

The old sailors reputation of a girl in every port is, for the most part unwarranted. There were, of course, those who were unable to keep it in their trousers when away from home, but for the most part, the crew were too intoxicated ashore to have been able to perform the sexual act. At sea however, with no beer available, it was a different matter. The urges returned. Now, if you are of a weak disposition, you may want to skip the next paragraph or so as I intend to talk about 'wankerchiefs'. Yes, you read it correctly, it began with a W. Masturbation is the subject.

The normal urges for sexual relief do not disappear just because a man is beneath the water for several weeks, or sometimes months, at a time. The only method of relief is what the Victorians called 'self abuse'. As I have said before, privacy on a submarine is virtually non existent. The only space a man has to himself at any time is his bunk. Now, a naval submarine bunk is particularly cramped, being about six feet long, two and a half feet wide and with another bunk only twelve inches above and below. If you imagine a coffin on its side with a curtain instead of a lid, you should have in your minds eye a picture of a submarine bunk. The actual act of masturbation could cause some considerable disruption in the bunk space. The squeaking of the bed alone could annoy anyone within earshot. And then there is the real problem of what to do with the residue. This is where wankerchiefs come into the equation. Each man would have a piece of material, about a foot square with which to wipe away the resultant mess. The wankerchief, in between uses, would be stowed in the only place available, under the mattress. This was fine for those on the top bunk, not quite so convenient for those beneath. The man on the bottom bunk of three might wake up with three wankerchiefs spread over his sleeping bag. Which one is his? Not a pleasant thought I know, but wankerchiefs were a necessary evil.

About three days out of Gibraltar, I was laying on my bunk reading. I could hear the noise of self abuse coming from the bunk across the passageway. It continued for some time until, with a subdued gasp, it came to what was obviously a satisfactory conclusion for the man involved.

There was a few seconds of silence followed by a loud exclamation.

"Alright, who's nicked me wankerchief?"

There were several fits of giggling from around the torpedo compartment as the conspirators struggled to contain their mirth.

"Come on boys, give us me wankerchief back, its all over me chest."

There was uproar.

"Right, you bastards."

I looked through the small crack in my curtains and could see the poor victim of the great wankerchief robbery laying on his bunk. As I watched I saw him look around in the gloom. The compartment was lit by only a small red light so as not to ruin the night vision of watchkeepers who may be required to act as lookout or take a spell on the periscope. He reached out of his bunk. Each of us had a towel draped over the end of our bunk to wipe away the sweat after a six hour stint of watchkeeping in the hot atmosphere of the engine room. The abuser took a towel off of the bunk next to his and deftly wiped away the residue from his chest. Cleansed he returned the towel and turned over to sleep. 'That's a bit off.' I thought, after all, it wasn't even his towel. I continued to read and, about an hour later, I heard someone walking up the center of the compartment between the rows of bunks. I again looked out through the crack in my curtains to see a large, heavily bearded marine engineer. He was dressed in overalls and sweating profusely, having been working in the engine room for the previous six hours. He stopped next to his bunk and stretched. He reached down and took his towel off of the end of his bunk, the same towel previously used by the self abuser. I watched in horror as he used the towel to wipe the sweat from his face and neck. Even in the gloom of the red light I could see a myriad of white sticky deposits in his beard. I was trying desperately not to laugh. Others in the compartment weren't managing as well as me in containing their laughter and I could hear spluttering and coughing from several nearby bunks.

For two days the unfortunate engineer was walking around the boat wondering why people were grinning at him. Nobody had the courage to tell him that his beard may become pregnant if he didn't wash it soon.

I was very careful with my wankerchief. I kept it securely hidden from possible burglars. It's a very personal thing, a man's wankerchief.

CHAPTER TWELVE

The exercise was fairly mundane and, with a sense of anticipation, Courageous and its crew headed deep into the Mediterranean for its next run ashore, Corfu. The Greek islands were about to play host to the pride of the Royal Navy.

The pure white houses, the blue sea and the sun. All I'd heard about the island of Corfu appeared to be true. I was standing on my hotel balcony overlooking Corfu Town. It was a hard life in the Navy, but someone had to do it. I hand a hand full of Drachma and a stomach devoid of beer. What was I to do? Oh, well, let's go and see what the island has to offer.

There was a loud bang on the door.

"Chas, are you coming out for a drink?"

I opened the door and there was Dave Harwood.

"Come on, the bars are open." He said, waving a wad of notes under my nose.

"Yeah, let me just get my shoes on and I'll be with you."

I followed him out of the hotel to where several of the crew were sitting outside the bar next door. There were tables on the pavement and they were occupied, in the most part, by submariners, desperate for drink. There was already quite a pile of empty glasses on the tables, the majority of them spirit glasses. I joined them and before I could even settle into one of the chairs, a glass of evil smelling alcohol appeared in front of me. It was ouzo, the local aniseed spirit. I threw it back in one. Jeeesus. Some sod had spiked it with petrol.

"Nice, ain't it?" Said one of the lads.

I couldn't speak, my throat was on fire and somebody had stolen the oxygen from the atmosphere. My eyes were streaming and my voice had gone.

"Here, have another one before we go."

Dave put another glass of the evil fluid on the table in front of me and looked at me with a grin. My speaking capabilities were slowly returning.

"Yeah, I'll drink it in a minute Dave." I said.

"Come on then, we're going down the noddy shop."

I looked at him. "The what?" I asked.

"The noddy shop, you've got to have a noddy to get about here." He replied.

I threw the drink back and, again, I suffered a massive stroke. My legs and lungs refused to work. I struggled to my feet.

"Lead on MacDuff." I said, trying to look nonchalant. He began to walk off and I followed. I tripped over the leg of a chair and went hurtling into a table full of young female holidaymakers. My face buried itself into the ample cleavage of a well built blonde. She screamed.

"Jesus Chas, can't you wait?" said Dave, hauling my face out of her breasts.

"Sorry love," he said to the girl, "He's been at sea for ten days and he can't help himself. He was a rapist before he joined the navy."

The girl looked at me as though I was something rather nasty on the bottom of her shoe.

"Just keep the dirty bastard away from me or I'll kick him in the bollocks." She said in a broad Birmingham accent.

I tried to explain that it was all an accident but, by the look in her eyes, she wouldn't have believed me anyway. Dave hauled me away and I managed to steady myself. I could finally see again and I staggered off with him and the others to the noddy shop, whatever that was.

About five minutes walk away we turned into one of the back streets. There on the pavement was a whole array of gleaming mopeds, the famous noddies.

"Here we are then Chas." Said Dave. "Pick your steed and we'll go for a spin.

I looked at the motorcycles before me. I had never ridden anything other than a bicycle. I hadn't got a clue how to ride one of those.

"I can't Dave, I haven't got a licence." I stuttered.

"You don't need a licence to drive one of these. They'll hire 'em to any bugger." He replied and ran into the middle of the display, touching and tweaking everywhere, looking for his favourite.

All around me were sailors, some of them barely able to stand, running around like children in a sweet shop.

"Oooh, this one's got mirrors."

"No, I want this one, it's got a go-faster stripe on the tank."

"I want one with a hooter."

"Here, look at this, it's got a pillion."

I reluctantly walked into the center of the bikes and looked around. How hard could it be to ride one of these things, after all they're only bicycles with a little engine.

A Greek chap was standing in the doorway. I'm sure he was rubbing his hands. He could see drachmas everywhere he looked.

I reluctantly chose a small green moped and signed a form, which was written in Greek. I could have been admitting to murder for all I knew. I couldn't understand a word of it, even the letters made no sense, let alone the words. A set of keys was thrust into my hand and I pushed the moped into the road. I switched it on and kicked the starting lever. It purred into life. All around me were drunken men astride their mopeds. As they started them the air around us became a blue haze of exhaust fumes. Bikes were being revved up on all sides. Slowly, the group began to move off, about twenty mopeds in convoy. I managed to get mine moving, this wasn't too difficult after all.

I don't know what side of the road we were supposed to be driving on but, just to make sure someone got it right we were taking up the whole width of the tarmac. There were mopeds weaving about all over the place. I saw a junction ahead and I gently applied the brakes. Nothing happened. I pulled harder on the levers and still it had no effect. I was hurtling toward the junction at fifteen miles an hour and I couldn't bloody stop. I flew past Dave who obviously had brakes that worked.

"Go for it Chas, show them how it's done." He cried over my shoulder.

The junction loomed ahead and my bike wasn't slowing down. I stuck my feet down, forgetting that I only had sandals on. My toes scraped along the road removing the top layers of skin. Still the bike continued. I entered the junction still doing ten miles an hour. Out of the corner of my eye I could see a large lorry heading straight for me. There was a large blast from its horn and it swerved round me. I shut my eyes and sailed across the junction with cars all around. Slowly the bike came to a halt and I got off, shaking and sweating. I looked back and there was chaos. About ten mopeds were on the road, there were drunken sailors falling about all over the place and irate Greek drivers threatening violence. They were beginning to square up to each other and then, over the sound of the melee we heard the engine of a single moped. It was screaming at full revs, working hard. I looked through the crowd and could see a small red bike coming toward the junction. Steering it was the Sonar Supervisor, a chief petty officer who weighed about eighteen stone. On the pillion was the Chief Stoker who was slightly the heavier, at about nineteen and a half stone. It was belching blue smoke and it was moving at about twenty miles per hour. The Sonar Supervisor was wearing a pair of welding goggles, which he had stolen from the boat, and a white silk scarf. He looked like a world war one fighter ace. As he approached the junction he went into his

Highway Code routine. He looked over his shoulder and, with his right hand, began to give the slowing down signal. The bike came to a sedate halt, tottered and fell over with a crash. He had forgotten to put his feet down to balance it. Both he and the Chief Stoker were pissed out of their brains. They lay on the dusty road giggling and trying to extricate themselves from the bent wreckage of the moped. The crowd in the middle of the junction were laughing so much they forgot to fight. Slowly, the crowd dispersed, leaving the two large senior rates, helpless with laughter, trying to right their trusty moped and restart it.

I decided enough was enough and I pushed my machine back to the noddy shop. I handed it back and walked away, a handful of drachma lighter but a fair bit wiser. Unfortunately, that didn't apply to many of the others.

Later that night I was sitting at the tables on the pavement bar, next to the hotel. Directly across from us was a tall bank of earth, a vertical drop of about ten feet from its top down to the road. The other side sloped gently down to an area of open land. As I was sitting, drinking a cold beer and enjoying a chat with some of the lads, the only thing that was marring the evening was the glances I was getting from the blonde bird from Birmingham. She obviously didn't like me much. I became aware of a humming noise in the background as we talked. It was getting louder. Slowly, the conversation dwindled as the hum became a moan and the moan became a scream. It was a moped, and it was coming closer. Because of the buildings it was difficult to determine which direction it was coming from. It became louder and louder and then, as we looked around, a moped came hurtling up the slope of earth on the other side of the road. It hit the top and took off. Crouched over the handlebars was Dave Harwood. He was flat out at about thirty two miles per hour when he hit the top and the bike flew across the road just above head height. It didn't take long for the people sitting at the tables to work out the trajectory and, in a mad scramble, bodies flew in all directions. Dave's gentle parabola cleared the road and gravity began to take over. The moped began to plummet earthward, heading straight for the tables where, until a few milliseconds before, we had been sitting. I dived for cover and, luckily, landed on something soft.

Looking round I saw Dave, complete with moped, hit the tables with a resounding crash. Plastic chairs and bits of table flew in all directions. There was a deathly silence, broken only by the sound of debris hitting the ground. From the middle of the chaos, Dave appeared, rising majestically from the dust cloud. His face had been laid open and there was a huge gash on his bare chest. He was covered in blood, which was pouring from several nasty wounds, which would obviously require stitches.

"I don't suppose they have valet parking here, do they?" he said, and collapsed on the ground in a heap.

I became aware of a woman screaming.

"Help, rape, rape."

I looked round. The soft thing that had broken my fall was the blonde bird from Birmingham. She was kicking and scratching me, convinced I was after her body. Thinking about it later, I was sure she was only upset because she thought I was after it without paying.

I'd had enough for one day and decided to go to bed. I couldn't, in all honesty, see this visit being another diplomatic coup for the Royal Navy.

CHAPTER THIRTEEN

The submarine was closed up at harbour stations, the Captain on the bridge and the crew ready to go. Just one snag, no Navigating Officer.

"Navigating Officer to the bridge." The Captain broadcast over the loudspeaker in the control room.

There was an ominous silence. The order was repeated and still no sign of a navigating officer. The sound powered telephone in the Control room bleeped and was answered by an unfortunate junior rating. There was a series of mumbled 'Yes sirs' and the phone was replaced in its cradle. The junior rate turned to the Petty Officer of the Watch.

"The Captain wants the Navigating Officer on the bridge, now." He said.

The Petty Officer of the Watch turned to the Officer of the Watch.

"Do you know where the Navigating Officer is sir?" he asked.

There was a blank look on the face of the young officer who hurriedly instigated a search of the wardroom but there was no sign of the elusive Navigating Officer. The Coxswain was enlisted to widen the search and the entire boat was quickly checked for signs of the missing officer. He reported back to the Officer of the Watch.

I was bridge lookout and I could see that the Captain was becoming impatient. He was drumming his fingers on the steel of bridge surround and becoming more and more angry as time slipped slowly by. We were now late sailing and the V.I.P.s, gathered on the jetty were beginning to become impatient.

The bridge speaker burst into life.

"Permission for the Officer of the Watch to come to the bridge, Captain?"

"Yes please." Came the abrupt reply.

The lieutenant climbed the ladder to the bridge and stood next to the Captain, whispering to him. There was an explosion as the Captain received the news.

"What do you mean, he's not on the boat? Where the hell is he?"

"Nobody knows sir, he was last seen in the hotel bar at one o' clock this morning."

The Captain's face was scarlet.

"Right, he'll have to fly back to the UK and take what's coming to him. I'm not waiting."

The Officer of the Watch left the bridge in an undignified rush and made his way below. The Captain gave the relevant orders and the submarine slipped from its berth and made its way back out to sea.

About twenty minutes out and the second bridge lookout reported a small contact, dead astern, making ground toward us. I swung my binoculars round to the relevant bearing and saw a small speedboat, the water creaming away from its bows in a white flurry. It was flat out and catching us fast.

"Watch and report." Ordered the Captain.

I continued to monitor the boat and, soon, I could see that the figure standing in the bows, hanging on for grim death and waving, was the Navigating Officer.

"Sir, the boat is continuing to close, I think it may want to come alongside." I reported. The Captain swung his binoculars onto the boat and went purple. The Navigating Officer was dressed in best bib and tucker, black bow tie included. He was waving a champagne bottle above his head.

The boat came alongside and the Navigating Officer made a leap onto the casing of the submarine. He was incredibly agile for one so obviously under the influence.

"Navigating Officer, get yourself into the correct dress of the day, and report to the bridge immediately. And bring the damned chart with you." The Captain said quietly. To me it sounded menacing. To the Navigator it was obviously a social invitation.

"Okey dokey, on my way." And he disappeared through the hatch into the submarine.

About five minutes later he reached the bridge. His white shirt looked as though it had been ironed with a breeze block and his tie was askew. He was grinning inanely as he handed the chart to the Captain. There isn't a great deal of room on the bridge of a submarine but it's amazing how much distance one can put between yourself and somebody who is so obviously in deep shit.

The Captain opened the chart.

"What's this Navigator?"

"It's a chart sir."

Yes, I know it's a chart. It's a chart of the Dover Straits." His voice was hushed and calm. Dangerous. The Navigator didn't seem to notice.

"Whoops. Silly me, wrong one." He said with a grin.

"Go below, get the correct chart, mark on it my planned course and return it to me on the bridge, at the rush."

"On me way boss." Replied the Navigator, with a snappy salute. He left the bridge, descending the ladder to the control room, whistling.

There was an awkward silence on the bridge, punctuated only by the reports of shipping contacts and the necessary acknowledgements by the Captain. After what seemed an age the Navigating Officer returned to the bridge. Someone had obviously had a word in his shell like ear. He was smartly dressed and had the correct chart with all the relevant information laid out neatly upon it. He handed it to the Captain and made his way to the back of the bridge, where he stood, swaying gently and trying not to giggle.

Ten minutes passed as the submarine made its way through the buoys marking the deep water shipping channel away from the island. The Captain was monitoring the progress on the chart and giving orders to the helmsman below to make small adjustments to the course.

"Navigator."

The inebriated officer jumped out of his skin. He had been half asleep in the warmth of the rising sun.

"Yes sir." He said, stepping forward to take up a position immediately behind the Captain, who pointed out to an area off of the starboard bow.

"That buoy isn't marked on the chart. What is it?" he asked quietly.

This was more than the Navigator could cope with. Without thinking he opened his mouth and issued the words that would later become legend on Courageous.

"How the hell should I know, I've never been here before."

I thought the Captain was going to physically assault him. Instead, he stormed below and ordered the Officer of the Watch to take the bridge. As he passed through the control room he ordered the Coxswain to "Get that bloody disgrace to the Royal Navy off my bridge and confine him to the Wardroom."

The Navigator spent a very lonely trip, shunned by his fellow officers, in whose eyes associating with him may have meant catching the highly infectious disease of disgrace. As soon as the submarine was, once more, in sight of land, the unfortunate officer was removed by fast launch and taken ashore. I never saw him again.

Whilst Courageous made its way back to the UK, I continued with my part three training. The training was governed by a book, containing a huge list of tasks that I was expected to be able to complete within a three month period. As a torpedo man I had to be able to have at least a basic working knowledge of every system on the ship and an in depth knowledge of any that I would be required to operate in my day to day duties aboard. I crawled around engine rooms, turbo generator rooms, the galley, I followed miles of pipework containing high pressure air, low pressure air, hydraulic fluid and sewage. I learnt to operate the air, hydraulic, ventilation, fresh water and salt water systems throughout the boat. On top of all this I had to learn my own job and pass exams and tests on the subject of the weapons, their storage, their preparation and firing. As a further distraction, I was required to qualify as a foreplanesman. During my watch in the control room I would have to steer the submarine and use the hydroplanes to change or maintain depth. It was like learning to fly a very slow and cumbersome aircraft, but without being able to look out of a window. The steering console, or two man band as it was called, was situated in the right hand forward corner of the control room. In the left hand seat sat a senior rate who controlled the after hydroplanes, which determined the angle of the submarine in the water. In the right hand seat was the foreplanesman who operated both the rudder and the forward hydroplanes. These, respectively controlled the course and depth of the boat. Behind the two man band, in a waist high barriered circle known as the bandstand, or playpen, stood the Officer of the Watch. He controlled the submarine whilst it was dived. To his right was the panel watchkeeper who sat before a large panel of switches and dials which controlled all the air, water and hydraulic systems required to keep the boat moving and safe. On the left hand side of the control room was the plotting table and fire control computers from where the boat was navigated across the oceans of the world and the weapons were fired and controlled when fighting. Behind and to the left of the Officer of the Watch were two periscopes, the binocular, wide headed search periscope and the smaller, monocular, attack periscope, which left a smaller wake on the surface when being used during the final stages of an attack. To ensure that the submarine could see and hear, in another enclosed section of the control room area, sat the sonar operators. They constantly swept the ocean for any sound, which may prove to be a danger to Courageous. The sounds of everything in the sea, from two hundred thousand ton super tankers to the crackle of shrimps and the patter of raindrops on the surface of the sea above, was heard in this room, categorized and either dismissed or acted upon. The boats eyes and ears needed to be in top condition at all times.

As night fell, the control room would go through several stages of lighting. In daylight, normal fluorescent light fittings were switched on. As dusk fell the submarine went to red lighting. All white lights would be switched off and the only light available would be small red light bulbs strategically placed around the submarine. It took on an eerie atmosphere. Colours became indistinguishable and everybody looked a very pale red. As darkness fell, the officer on the periscope would become sensitive to the smallest pinprick of light, which could ruin his night vision. To prevent this occurring the submarine went to black lighting. All lights were switched off in the control room and blackout curtains were rigged at all entrances to prevent even the smallest amount of light from entering. Movement in the control room was by instinct and touch, only the instruments on the steering console having the smallest of backlights. All torches carried had to have a dark red filter across the lens and any light entering the control room was greeted with shouts and insults.

Watchkeepers from the control room who took a short break to get a cup of tea, or have a cigarette, were required to wear dark red goggles when they left the control room so that, if the alarm was sounded, they could dash back to their watchkeeping position without having lost their ability to see.

All of this was still new and strange to me. Little was I to know that I would spend the next twelve and a half years living in this world. But, for now, I had to study. The Captain, or First Lieutenant, personally examined all part three trainees before they were deemed to be fully qualified submariners. My exam had been scheduled for the day before we entered UK waters. I had a lot to learn, and not a great deal of time to learn it in. If I failed the exam I risked suffering from stoppage of submarine pay. My one pound forty four pence a day could be lost. At the time, my basic weekly wage had risen astronomically to thirty two pounds a fortnight, a huge rise from the seven pounds a fortnight I had earned when I first joined the Navy. That one pound forty four pence was a huge sum to me and I didn't intend to lose it.

Luckily the trip home was uneventful and, whenever I was off watch, I was able to study. I only slept for about three hours a day for the next ten days, but, when the time came, I intended to be ready.

The day of reckoning was upon me. I had obtained a signature from each head of department in my training schedule and I had carried out a thousand tasks to prove that I knew the ship like the back of my hand. After all, if the chef fell overboard or the engineer became ill, someone had to feed the crew and keep the engines going.

I reported to the First Lieutenant's cabin at the prearranged time. I had never been so nervous in my life. If I failed I would take some stick, that much was certain. If I passed I would be accepted as a member of the crew. In the corner of the cabin was a full set of breathing apparatus, used by the crew to fight fires in smoke filled compartments.

"Good morning, Cooke. Put that on for me, there's a good chap." Said the Jimmy, as the First Lieutenant was always known.

I struggled into the set, two large oxygen bottles on my back secured by shoulder and waist straps. It weighed about sixty five pounds.

"If you'd like to put on the face mask, we'll make a start." The Jimmy said.

I picked the face mask up. It was connected to the oxygen bottles by a long rubber hose and the mask covered the whole face. The Perspex sight-glass in the mask had been covered in thick black masking tape. I put it on and was immediately blind.

"Right then, off we go. Take me to the emergency propulsion motor." Demanded the Jimmy.

Now the wardroom, (officer's mess), was at the front of the boat, the emergency propulsion motor was as far away as it was possible to go, right back in the motor room, by the propeller. It was through the control room, in which people were working, across the top of the reactor compartment through what was known as the tunnel, and then through all of the engineering spaces. Off we went. I could hear the giggles of the rest of the crew as I groped my way aft. I bumped into people who had been directed not to help or move out of my way. I groped for handles to open hydraulically operated watertight doors and I bounced my head off of a number of strategically placed sharp protrusions throughout the boat. Finally, I reached the motor room and placed my hand on the top of the emergency propulsion motor.

"Very good Cooke. Now, I want you to show me the main vent for number six main ballast tank. Off we went again.

"Now show me the turbo generator."

Now I want to go to the toilet, take me to the senior rates bathroom and heads."

"I'm hot, take me to the galley, I need a drink of water."

You're not the only one, I thought, but off I went.

Take me to the electrolyser space."

"Take me to the auxiliary machinery space." On and on it went. I had been crawling around the boat like a mad mole for the best part of two hours.

"Take me to the junior rate's mess."

I climbed down another ladder and groped my away along the passageway for the third time and made my way into the mess.

"You can take the mask off now, Cooke." Said the Jimmy.

I removed the mask, blinking in the bright light of the mess. There was every single off watch member of the crew. On the table in front of me was a glass of rum. In the bottom of the glass I could see something glinting. It was a submariner's badge, two gold dolphins, face to face with the royal crown between them.

"Congratulations, you are now a qualified submariner and a full member of the crew of Her Majesty's Submarine Courageous." Said the Jimmy with a smile. He patted me on the back of my sweat soaked shirt and the Coxswain handed me the glass of rum. To the cheers of the other men present, I threw the rum back in one, catching the coveted badge in my teeth. I was qualified. I was no longer a trainee and I could keep my one pound and forty four pence per day submarine pay. I had never felt so proud in my life.

CHAPTER FOURTEEN

Courageous entered the Gareloch in its normal fashion, a fully rigged out Scottish piper on the after casing, playing the bagpipes. We tied up alongside and there was a mad dash to get ready to go ashore. We had to get customs clearance first and Her Majesty's Customs and Excise representative came aboard.

Every member of the crew was required to complete a declaration form listing the items bought abroad and which they were bringing back into the UK. It was amazing how the whole crew declared exactly twenty pounds worth of gifts, that being the precise amount permitted into the country without incurring excise duty. No matter how often or how hard they searched the submarine, the Customs Officers never managed to find the hidden booty. One of the favourite tricks was to hide presents in an empty torpedo tube. On the rear door of the torpedo tube was a plate with the legend, 'loaded with Mk 24 Warshot'. The tube rear door had a small drain cock on it, used to test the tube for water before opening. A large bottle of sea water was placed on the inside of the door and connected to the inner surface of the drain cock. If the customs officer asked to look in the torpedo tubes he would be shown those that were empty. If he asked to look in the one in which the presents were stowed he would be politely refused and informed that it was loaded with a live torpedo and the tube flooded. The duty torpedoman would then open the drain cock and a spurt of seawater would squirt out of it, generally over the customs officer's trousers. He would leave, happy in the knowledge that there was nothing but a torpedo, containing eight hundred pounds of explosive, stowed in the tube. No sooner had the customs officer left the boat than the tube door would be opened, the bottle removed and the illicit presents returned to their rightful owners. I hope they don't still use that trick or I could be costing a lot of submariners a great deal of money on their next return to the UK.

I was going on a long weekend leave while the submarine started an extended maintenance period. I could hardly wait to get away and, as soon as the Coxswain obtained permission from the Captain, he piped leave to those entitled. I was over the gangway like a rat up a drainpipe. Freedom.

I had arranged to go and visit my brother, who was the manager of a supermarket in Aldershot. It was a long journey but I had my railway travel warrant in my hand. I shared a taxi with three other lads off of the boat and made my way to Helensburgh station. From there, a half hour train trip and I was in Glasgow. I had a last pint with the lads in the city before making my way to Glasgow Central Station and catching the train south.

It was a five hour journey and it was almost nine o clock before the train pulled into Euston Station. I made my way across the underground and, having reached Waterloo, managed to catch a slow train to Aldershot. It was almost eleven pm before I reached Ray's flat above the shop and I was exhausted. Ray had only recently been married and he and his wife, Paula, had not long had their first child. I slept on the sofa in the living room and, as soon as my head touched the pillow, I was asleep.

I woke, at about nine thirty the following morning, to the sound of cups rattling in the kitchen. Paula was making tea and I quickly washed and dressed before sitting down to a refreshing cuppa. I told her about my trip and she spoke of their new son, Rory. It was nice to feel part of a real family again. Ray had left home at fifteen, as had I two years later, and we had, for the most part gone our separate ways. We had seen very little of each other for the last two or three years, not that we didn't get on, we just had our own lives to lead.

I was later to have reason to be glad that I had managed to catch up with Ray and get to know him as my older brother. He was to contract motor neuron disease at the age of thirty six, and I was there when he passed away a week after his fortieth birthday. I have since come to treasure every moment we had spent together and I only wish he could have lived to read this book. It would have made him laugh, I'm sure.

I finished my tea and chatted with Paula for a while before going downstairs to the shop, to see Ray and give him a hand if it was needed. We unloaded a delivery from a lorry and then sat down for another cup of tea. We got to talking.

"Have you got a girlfriend yet?" Ray asked.

"No, not yet, I don't seem to have the time really." I replied.

"Well, you know what they say about you sailors." Came the obvious retort.

"It's nothing like that, I just haven't had the time, what with all my training and being at sea."

Ray nodded his head in the direction of the shop floor.

"Why don't you ask Caroline?" he said.

"No. she won't want to go out with a sailor, not in Aldershot, they all go for the squaddies, don't they?"

"Not Caroline, she'll go out with anything in trousers."

I looked through the door of the stockroom and could see the girl in question working on the shop floor. I thought she was beautiful. Long brown hair, blue eyes and a figure to die for. It really was love at first sight.

He looked at me and winked.

"Go on." Ray encouraged.

I sauntered out to the shop floor and, to this day, I can't remember what I said. It must have worked because Caroline agreed to go out with me that evening.

Later, I met Caroline at her home and we walked to a local pub for a drink. As we entered the pub was fairly quiet and I selected a table in the corner of the bar. I am, or at least I was then, fairly shy. Caroline was drinking vodka and lime and I was slinging pints down my neck to build up the Dutch courage. We seemed to be comfortable with each other and we began to chat like old friends. I couldn't believe how beautiful she was. Then the beer began to take effect. I was suffering from the 'drink one piss six syndrome'. I excused myself and almost ran to the gent's toilet to relieve my aching bladder.

On my return to the bar, something had changed. Caroline was still sitting at the table where I had left her but the entertainment for the night had arrived. An elderly man had set up his stall right next to our table. He had a piano accordion and the biggest loudspeaker I had ever seen. As I settled back into my seat he began to play. My right eardrum immediately hit the left hand side of my skull as the loudspeaker burst into life. Good God. I had never heard a piano accordion played through a loudspeaker, and I hope never to do so again. Speech became impossible and the rest of the evening was conducted in sign language, punctuated by my regular dash to the toilet. I had a bladder like a space hopper and I was permanently busting for a pee. I have no idea what Caroline thought at the time and she has never told me. I don't think I want to know.

Eventually closing time was upon us and I escorted Caroline home, where she lived with her widowed mother. We kissed goodnight and I was hooked. I walked back to Ray's flat in a daze.

I didn't see Caroline the following day as it was Sunday and the shop was shut. I spent a pleasant morning with Ray and Paula but really I was thinking, all the while, about Caroline. It was soon time for me to leave. I had to catch the overnight train back to Scotland. I said goodbye to Ray and Paula and made my way to the train station. For the first time since joining the Navy, I didn't want to go back.

At Euston Station I went to the bookstall and bought myself a pen and writing pad. I boarded the train to Glasgow and settled down for the long journey north. It was a busy train, but I had learned a few tricks in the navy and one of those was how to get a compartment to yourself. I boarded early and walked along the passageway until I found an empty compartment. I slid the door shut behind me and pulled down the blinds on the windows facing the aisle. I took from my holdall a small can of vegetable soup, that I had purchased in Ray's shop before I left and, using a ration pack can opener, removed the lid. Slowly I poured the vegetable soup in a small heap on the floor of the compartment and, having taken off my shoes, I laid down on the seat to sleep. It didn't take long. The door slid open and a middle aged, well dressed woman with husband and two children stood in the doorway. I looked at her through half closed eyelids and muttered something completely unintelligible, finishing off with a loud belch. She looked around to her husband.

"Disgusting man," she said, "he's drunk, and he's been sick on the floor. We'll find somewhere else to sit, come along." And with that she closed the door and went off in search of alternative seating. That trick stood me in good stead over the years of traveling between Euston and Glasgow. It never failed and I always managed to get a good night's sleep on my journey back to Faslane.

I spent the next five days working on the boat in a daze. I was in love and, thinking back, I must have been a right pain in the arse. All my spare time was spent in my room, in the barracks, writing two or three letters a day to Caroline.

As Friday approached I became more and more impatient and finally the time came when I could once again make the long journey south. The company that owned Ray's shop was holding its annual dinner dance on the Saturday, a rather posh affair at The Holborn Hotel with the marching band of the Coldstream Guards as part of the cabaret, and Caroline was going. I had managed to wangle an invitation.

Once again I stayed at Ray's flat in Aldershot and after arriving late on the Friday night, spent Saturday in the shop, helping Caroline with her work and mooning over her in the staff rest room, drinking tea. The working day ended and I walked Caroline home where I left her to get ready for the night out. We met again on the coach to London and I sat next to her on the journey. We talked as though we had known each other for years and finally I turned to her and said,

"When are we getting married then?"

"How about a year today?" She replied looking me straight in the eyes.

"Are you serious?" I asked.

"Yes, of course I am." She said with a smile.

We were engaged. I had known Caroline for one week of which we had been together for a total of about four hours. It was the eleventh of October 1975 and the closest Saturday to that in a years time was the ninth. We sat there, on the coach, discussing the wedding plans and opted for that date. On arrival at the function we sat together and announced our engagement to Ray and Paula. Ray looked as though someone had pole axed him; Paula just smiled and congratulated us both.

It was exactly a year later that we married. We had actually managed to be together for a grand total of ten days in the year and we were virtual strangers the day we married, but twenty nine years later and we are still together.

Right, enough of the romance, back to the tales. I am sure Caroline won't mind.

CHAPTER FIFTEEN

The wind was bitterly cold and the rain was beginning to turn to sleet. I was on the bridge as we made our way slowly down the Gareloch, toward Rhu Narrows and out to sea again. I was wearing my white roll necked submarine sweater under my foul weather gear and I was still cold. The waterproof jacket was specially designed to funnel water down the neck and did nothing to help keep out the cold. I couldn't wait to fall out from harbour stations and go below again, into the warm muggy atmosphere of the boat. I could smell the aroma of food coming up through the hatch from the galley below where the cooks were preparing a brunch for the crew. The beginning of another trip. This time we were to patrol for four weeks, sneaking about the oceans, helping to subdue the evil red menace. After the patrol we were to be rewarded with a run ashore in Torquay. Who in the Admiralty planned the ships programme I had no idea but, they could at least have sent us there in the summer months when the town was still full of holidaymakers and, at least a part of the population would be under eighty five years of age.

Just as I thought that I would never be warm again the watch was ordered to patrol routine and I was allowed to leave the bridge. I dived below and grabbed a large plate full of chops, egg, steak, bacon, beans and chips. The crew immediately began to settle into the six hours on, six hours off routine of life at sea and, already, only a few hours after sailing, men were climbing into sleeping bags to sleep.

It was a tradition in the submarine service that on one day, approximately half way through a patrol, each mess would have a mess dinner. It was the crew's opportunity to return to a civilized way of life for a few hours. The galley provided a meal of steak with all the trimmings and the mess members sat down together, as much as the watch system would allow, to eat. The Senior Rates wore white shirt and tie while the wardroom went the whole hog. Officers would dress in mess undress, complete with bow tie, the silverware would be brought out of storage and the stewards would distribute the food with silver service being the order of the day. The morning after the mess dinner had taken place I was talking to George the steward. We were in chimney corner, a small space at the rear of the control room, and at the top of the ladder down to the mess decks and bunk spaces below, where watchkeepers were allowed to go for a cigarette without being far away from their allotted position.

Charlie Hammersley, a lieutenant and ship's general dogs body officer, appeared around the corner from the control room.

"Ah, George, just the man." He said, "I want to see you in the lower level of the torpedo compartment at 1900 this evening."

"Okay sir." Replied George, looking at the officers retreating backside with a puzzled expression. Lieutenant Hammersley stopped and turned back.

"Oh, and George, wear sports kit." He said before continuing down the ladder and out of sight.

"What's that about then George?" I asked.

"Buggered if I know Chas. Mind you, I am coming up for my annual appraisal so that's probably it."

"Yeah, but what's all that about sports kit?" I enquired.

"I haven't got a clue mate. Mind you, Charlie's a bit mad, he probably wants to give me a fitness test or something knowing him. He plays rugby for the Navy doesn't he, they're all bloody mad, those rugby players."

George stubbed out his cigarette and returned to the wardroom to continue his cleaning of the officer's bunk spaces.

I wandered back into the control room to take over the helm. The Sonar Officer was the Officer of the Watch in the bandstand and I requested permission to relieve the helm. Permission having been given I slid into the seat and took a note of the ship's course, depth and speed.

"Cooke, have you met our midshipman yet?"

I looked over my left shoulder. The Sonar Officer was beckoning to a midshipman, a trainee officer, who looked as though his mother should know he was out. He was about two years older than me and was still pink and freshly scrubbed from Dartmouth Naval College. I had seen him about the boat but he appeared to be painfully shy and, as yet, I hadn't spoken to him or him to me.

"No sir, I haven't." I said.

The young midshipman walked across the control room and I was introduced. He was nervous and had, obviously, been warned of submariners and their strange behaviour. We spoke about life aboard and he was beginning to warm to the conversation. He seemed pleasant enough.

"Right you officers, whose is this bugger?" It was George. He was standing in the middle of the control room, between the periscopes, waving a condom around in his left hand. He was throwing accusing looks at all the officers in the control room. I saw the Captain peer from behind the curtains around the chart table, a puzzled expression on his face at the commotion now under way in his control room.

"Right," exclaimed George. "I have here, in my sticky mitt, a condom, found under a bunk in the officer's sleeping quarters." He held it out for all to view. "As you can see, there are deposits within said condom and the top has been neatly tied up to prevent leakage of the contents."

He pointed to the deposit sitting in the end of the condom and to the knot securing the open end.

"I want to know which of you Ruperts has been having a posh wank." George continued. He strolled around the control room, addressing each officer in turn.

"Is this yours sir?" He asked them, receiving refusals from all concerned.

Finally he approached the midshipman and waved the condom under his nose. The young officer retreated from the flailing latex and shrunk into the corner behind my seat. I turned to watch the fun.

"Now then, sir," said George, "I found this under the top bunk of three on the starboard side of the six man bunk space. Where do you sleep?"

The midshipman had turned a deep shade of scarlet.

"That's my bunk." He said as George waved the offending condom directly under his nose.

"Aha!" exclaimed George, "I thought as much, it's yours, isn't it? Didn't your Mother tell you, masturbation will make you go blind?"

The midshipman was mortified, he was almost in tears by now, embarrassed and trapped in a corner by a mad fat steward with an offensive French letter.

"It's not mine, it's not mine I tell you." He said, in a trembling voice.

George looked him in the eye and raised an eyebrow.

"Let's see if you're telling the truth, shall we?"

Quickly, he untied the knot of the condom, put the open end to his lips and tipped the contents of the condom into his open mouth. He rolled the fluid around his mouth like a connoisseur of fine wine, gargled it in the back of his throat and swallowed loudly. By this time the midshipman was retching into a handkerchief and had gone deathly white. George looked up at him and smiled.

"I do apologise, you're absolutely right, that was the Captain's sperm." He said, turned and walked away to the wardroom.

The midshipman extricated himself from his corner and ran from the control room, handkerchief over his mouth, attempting to hold back the vomit until he reached the safety of the officers' toilet. How was he to know George had put condensed milk into the condom?

By the grins on the faces of the Captain and other officers, they had put George up to this. Even officers are allowed to have a sense of humour you know, no matter how sick it may be.

Later that evening I was sitting in the torpedo compartment, reading the latest tuppenny blood paperback book from the ship's library, a rather grandly named bookshelf in the second coxswain's store. I was in my normal position, just inside the watertight door on the convenient step. I was facing the front of the boat and before me was the narrow passageway between the rows of bunks on either side. To my right was the small hatch, leading down to the lower level where the torpedo tubes were situated and the torpedoes and mines were stored in their racks.

"Good evening Cooke, excuse me please."

I turned around and saw Lieutenant Hammersley. He was resplendent in a crisp, white singlet, navy blue shorts, and plimsoles and, I did a double take at this item, a pair of ancient brown leather boxing gloves. He had, under his arm, a second, equally ancient pair of gloves, fisticuffs for the use of. I moved to one side and he moved past me and, with some difficulty, due to the boxing gloves, descended the ladder into the lower level. Shiner Wright, the on watch torpedoman came aft from his position at the front of the compartment.

"Chas, tell me I am hallucinating. Please, tell me that wasn't Charlie in boxing gloves."

"'Fraid so Shiner. He wanted George to meet him in the lower level at 1900. George seemed to think it was his annual write up, but looking at Charlie I think George is in for a surprise."

A few minutes passed and we could hear Charlie prancing about the lower level. Looking through the grating deck from directly above, we could see him energetically shadow boxing his way around the tube space, sweating profusely.

"Alright lads, what's worth looking at then?"

"Nothing really George," said Shiner with a slight grin, "I think Charlie's waiting below to do your appraisal."

"Oh, right. He's early. I'd better get down there then." Said George as he hauled his considerable bulk down the ladder and disappeared from view, only to reappear below us. We had a bird's eye view through the grating.

Charlie stopped his shadow boxing and wiped his brow with the back of his not inconsiderable forearm. He reached out and, from beneath a torpedo, pulled the second pair of boxing gloves, which he threw to George.

"Put those on then steward." He ordered.

We could see the puzzled expression on George's face as he managed to clumsily catch the gloves.

"Come on then, I'm on watch in twenty minutes, can't keep the Captain waiting." Said Charlie impatiently.

"But I thought I was here for an appraisal sir, you are my Divisional Officer and it's just about due."

"That's next week, tonight I intend to teach you a lesson. Put the gloves on."

George, his mind by now befuddled by Charlie's antics, struggled into the boxing gloves. Charlie was now prancing around George in circles, feinting and ducking.

"Come on, put them up, defend yourself."

George looked even more puzzled and put his fists up in front of his chest. Charlie took that as the bell and launched a ferocious attack, two rapid punches to the midriff, which knocked the air out of George. He doubled over, wheezing and trying to catch his breath. Charlie struck out with a superbly executed right uppercut, which caught George plumb on the chin. His head snapped back and Shiner and I could actually see the lights go out in George's eyes. He crumpled to the deck. Charlie continued to prance.

"Had enough have you? That will teach you. Want some more? You ratings, you don't have a clue how to fight."

Shiner and I were stunned. An officer had struck a junior rating. It wasn't even in self-defence. He could be court martialled and we were witnesses.

George was beginning to stir. Groggily he opened his eyes and struggled to his knees, still winded from the body blows and dazed from the uppercut. He shook his head and looked up at Charlie who was above him.

"What the bloody hell did you do that for, sir?"

"I wanted to teach you a lesson George." Charlie replied. "Don't you ever give the Sonar Officer a bigger steak than me at the mess dinner again. Do you understand?"

George nodded as he knelt on the tiled deck.

"Good, now come along, I'll help you up and buy you a beer from the Wardroom bar." And with that, Charlie helped the recovering George from his prone position, pushed him up the ladder and they went off down the passageway together like bosom pals.

"Do you believe that, Chas?" Shiner asked, shaking his head in amazement. "Those two are bleedin' mad." He walked away, still muttering to himself and I returned to my book. For some strange reason I found it particularly hard to concentrate on the pages after that. Oh well, it takes all sorts to make the world go round. I just wished they weren't all in my world.

CHAPTER SIXTEEN

The patrol was drawing to a close. We had been away from our families and loved ones, with no contact whatsoever, for four weeks now. I had religiously written a few pages to Caroline three or four times a day since we had sailed. I had half a ream of paper, covered in my handwriting, under my mattress. It was beginning to become uncomfortable, trying to sleep on the resulting lump in the middle of the bed. We were looking forward to getting ashore, even if it was Torquay in the winter. At least, once ashore, we could post letters and use a phone.

"Standby to surface."
There was a rush of air into the ballast tanks and the bow tilted upward. The boat sprung from the depths and, as always, with the weight of the water still trapped in the fin, it heeled to starboard before righting itself.
"On the surface, open up." Ordered the Captain.
"The officer of the watch flung open the upper hatch of the conning tower and stepped out onto the bridge. As surfacing lookout I was right behind him. The cramped bridge at the top of the fin was still draining and water was slopping around our feet. A watery winter sun was shining and I had to squint. Four weeks of artificial light, without

seeing the outside world, takes its toll and some time elapses before a submariner is able to readjust to daylight and fresh air.

The sky was a clear pale blue and the sea was flat calm, only the disturbance caused by the boat as she had surfaced breaking the water into waves.

"Officer of the watch Captain, no visual contacts, the plant is in the half power state, course three four zero, revolutions for twenty knots. You have the submarine."

"I have the submarine, aye aye sir." The officer of the watch repeated. "Helm, bridge, steer three four zero, revolutions for twenty knots. Fall out from watch diving, hands to patrol routine."

The boat settled down on course and increased speed. A bow wave formed around the front of Courageous and, behind us, a large white wake began to form, as straight as an arrow. The sound of the water rushing past the hull was hypnotic and I began to relax, sweeping my binoculars around the horizon, which was empty as far as the eye could see. This time tomorrow and I would be ashore and speaking to Caroline.

The rattle of the anchor chain told us that we had arrived. There was not enough depth of water in any of the local harbours for Courageous and we were to anchor in the centre of Torbay. The navy had chartered a local tourist boat to take us ashore and bring us back and it was due to run a regular shuttle service between the boat and the shore.

As soon as we arrived we could see the local fishing boats heading out from the harbours to have a look at the sleek black messenger of death that was anchored just half a mile from their homes.

"Here, Chas, who was it that had those Russian hats and shirts?"

I turned round to see Pete Carmel, the second Coxswain.

"I'm not sure mate, they were loafing around the mess the other day and then they disappeared."

"If I can get hold of a couple in the next few minutes, do you fancy a bit of a laugh?"

"Go for it mate." I said, and Pete dashed below again with a grin on his face. He reappeared a few moments later with two blue and white hooped T-shirts, two dark blue tunics and two furry hats with a bright red Russian hammer and sickle emblem on the front.

"Here, stick these on." He said, throwing me one of each item of clothing. "And the only Russian you need to know for this is 'Dubrosky matros."

"What does that mean then?" I asked as I struggled into the offered outfit.

His face appeared, with a smile, from the top of the T-shirt.

"Hello sailor." He replied.

Other members of the crew had appeared to watch the fun. They were standing on the bridge at the top of the fin, peering over the edge, inside the fin door and out of the main access hatch.

As the first of the boats approached, the Torpedo Instructor popped out of the hatch, in his hands, two sub-machine guns from the ship's armoury. They were of course unloaded.

"Here you go boys, just for a bit of effect, and by the way, the Captain's watching through the periscope so don't go too far over the top."

He disappeared back down the hatch and Pete and I slung the menacing looking weapons over our shoulders and did our best to look menacing. We stood with our backs to the closing fishing boats and waited. The first boat soon came almost alongside and began a slow circuit around the submarine, the occupants, obviously a local fisherman and his family, looked at Courageous with interest.

Pete nudged me and we both turned around. The look on the fisherman's face as he focused on the sub-machine guns was a picture. His wife stepped back in the boat and slipped on something, falling, legs apart, into the bottom of the small vessel.

The fisherman's eyes moved up and caught a glimpse of the furry hats and I could see him struggling to focus on the badge in the centre of the brow. Dave waved and said something unintelligible which, to my untrained ear, sounded Russian. He nudged me and I lifted my arm and waved to the, by now, petrified fisherman.

"Dubrosky matros." I called in my best guttural Russian accent.

Pete lifted the sub-machine gun from his shoulder and waved it in the air toward the boat. The fisherman nearly had a heart attack.

"It's the bloody Russians." He shouted to his family over the sound of the boats diesel engine, which began to roar as the small craft heeled over in a hard turn and headed, at full speed, toward the remainder of the closing fleet of small vessels.

There was laughter from those watching and Pete and I quickly changed back into our normal submariners kit of white roll neck sweater and dark blue trousers. The Russian uniform was taken below and we waited patiently for the next boat to arrive. Our friend the fisherman had by now reached his townsfolk, about two hundred yards away and was obviously passing the news of the arrival of the red menace. Many of the boats turned around and headed back to shore. A few braver skippers decided to come and check out the impending peril for themselves. As they came closer Pete and I, by now joined by other crewmen, all looking very British were standing on the casing.

"Good afternoon, lovely day for the time of year." Pete called to the first of the boats.

The skipper looked puzzled.

"Are you English?" He asked from a safe distance.

"Yeah, of course we are. What made you ask that?" I called.

"One of our blokes said there were Russians on your deck with machine guns."

Pete laughed and lifted an imaginary bottle to his lips.

"He must have been in the pub too long mate, no Russians here." I said.

The boat skipper shook his head and waved, turning back toward the shore. No doubt our first visitor would be branded a lunatic alcoholic, and it was all our fault, but then, it was highly unlikely that we would ever give a toss, we had had a good laugh.

"Okay you two, enough is enough." It was the Captain who had appeared on the casing. "I've got to have dinner with the mayor tonight and I'm going to have to lie to him about this." He walked aft, chuckling. Courageous had arrived in Torbay.

The remainder of our first night passed reasonably quietly. I took the first available boat ashore, posted a whole bunch of letters, phoned Caroline and then spent the evening in an alcohol-induced daze in the pubs of Torquay before retiring to the bed and breakfast that several members of the crew had also booked into. It was a night for relaxing and winding down after the patrol. We were all too tired to cause any real trouble, although the local constabulary probably had their busiest night since the end of the summer season. On the whole it was good-natured and the local police were acting as submariner's taxis for the night, ferrying drunken sailors back to their hotels.

We tended to have a good relationship with the police, wherever we went in the UK. We always made a point of inviting them to visit the boat and have a few free beers with us onboard. It's always difficult to arrest someone who, only the night before, had bought you as much beer as you could drink and took you, drunk, back to your house. It wasn't so much corruption as a localized form of diplomatic relations. Well, that's the way we saw it.

On the second day of our four in Torbay, I was duty. I wasn't particularly looking forward to it. The Captain, having dined at the Mayoral reception the previous night, was duty bound to host a cocktail party onboard the boat. As duty watch we had to be on our best behaviour. We spent the day cleaning and polishing until the boat gleamed from stem to stern. All the secret equipment or sensitive items of shipboard hardware were covered in colourful flags and bunting. The wardroom was resplendent with the mess silver, brought out for this special occasion.

As the wardroom was so small the control room would also form part of the area in which the Captain would entertain his guests. This made life a little difficult for the duty watch, as they had to continue to monitor the ship's systems, many of them situated in the control room itself. That meant that we also had to be in our best uniform for the duration of the function. The casing sentry, in best bib and tucker, spent his entire watch on deck, greeting dignitaries and helping them in and out of a rocking boat onto the slippery and narrow casing. Getting the guests down the vertical access hatch was a favourite job. The sailor at the bottom had the opportunity to look straight up the cocktail dress of any female guest who had chosen to ignore the advice in relation to trousers being the most practical form of dress for boarding a submarine.

I was on watch in the control room, trying to concentrate on monitoring the many gauges and dials on the ship's systems panel. I was surrounded by men and women of all ages, dressed up to the nines, drinking cocktails.

"Psst. Chas."

I turned around to see Bert Jameson, the forward stoker for the night, poking his head into the control room from Chimney Corner. He beckoned to me and I walked across.

"What's the matter Bert?" I asked.

"The shit tank's nearly full, and this lot ain't helping. I'm going to have to blow it overboard." He said. "Can you get hold of the duty officer and ask permission to do it?"

I nodded and re-entered the control room, searching for the Torpedo Officer, who was the duty Rupert. I found him deep in conversation with a buxom young lady in a miniscule top. She had nipples like Scammel wheel nuts and the officer's eyes were glued to them.

"Excuse me sir, could I have a quick word please?" I asked.

He looked at me, reluctantly dragging his eyes from the young lady's bust. I must admit, I found them to be quite impressive as well. I thought to myself, if she's selling those two puppy's she's got inside her shirt, I'll have the one with the red nose.

"Well, what is it Cooke?"

I snapped back to the real world.

"The sewage tank is full, permission to carry on and blow it overboard please sir?"

"Yes, of course, but make all the normal warnings." He replied and immediately went back to perusing the woman's cleavage. It would appear that I was dismissed.

I wandered back through the control room and found Bert, still waiting at Chimney Corner.

"The duty officer says to go ahead, but don't forget to make the warning broadcast."

"Cheers mate." Said Bert and disappeared down the ladder to prepare things.

Now, I may need to explain a few facts of submarine life here, especially in relation to the toilet facilities. For every two feet of depth to which a submarine dives, the external pressure on the hull increases by one pound per square inch. So, at six hundred feet, the external pressure is, approximately, three hundred pounds per square inch, an awful lot of pressure, when you take into account the surface area of the submarine hull.

I defy anybody in this world to eject, from his or her bodily orifices, any item of human waste at that pressure. If any reader knows of anyone who can do so, please let me know, as I would like to put them on the stage and be their agent. To overcome this problem, all the sinks drains and toilets on Courageous were drained into the slop drain and sewage tank, a large holding tank in the bottom of the boat. Once every 24 hours, normally at night, the contents would be blown over the side. This was quite an involved evolution during which all the sinks and toilets had to be isolated from the tank and a low pressure air blow being routed into the tank. Once the pressure in the tank was higher than the sea pressure outside a hull valve was opened and the contents would be pushed out into the sea.

There are several inherent problems with this system. Firstly, the toilets and sinks are out of use throughout the period that the tank is being blown. Secondly, if the boat is at sixty feet, the tank pressure must exceed thirty pounds per square inch or the seawater will flow into the tank instead of the contents going out. Thirdly, when the tank is emptied the air used to blow it must not be allowed to go through the hull valve or large bubbles would reach the surface to give away the boats position. Finally, once the tank is emptied and the hull valve is shut, the air inside the tank is still at thirty pounds per square inch. The pressure must be released somewhere and the only place for it to go is back into the boat. The result is a six hundred gallon fart, which permeates throughout the boat, adding to the already pungent aroma of sweaty men and cooked food.

Back to the story.

About five minutes later Bert reappeared at my shoulder.

"Almost ready Chas, just got a few more valves to shut and I've got to make the warning broadcast. I might as well do that now while I'm here."

Bert walked across to the broadcast system control box in the deckhead above the helmsman's seat and picked it up. He put all the switches down, making sure that the broadcast would be heard throughout the entire submarine. He put the microphone to his lips and, in his deep cockney voice announced,

"Do you hear there, bogs and bathrooms out of use, lining up to blow the shit tank overboard."

There was silence around him as the cocktail party conversation stuttered to a halt. He replaced the microphone in its holder and turned to leave.

"Jameson." It was the Captain. "We have guests aboard, moderate your language and hurry up with the blow."

The Captain was obviously embarrassed and angry at Bert's terminology and Bert was now panicking. He had upset the Captain, the last thing you should do on a submarine. He was God onboard and could dole out some particularly awful punishments if he was of a mind to be vindictive.

"Sorry sir, I wasn't thinking." Bert said apologetically and scuttled out of the control room.

I returned to the systems panel and continued my watch. There was a nagging worry at the back of my mind, but I couldn't figure out what it was. I sat there, trying to think what the problem was. I scanned the panel for any sign of a problem with the ship's systems.

Trim system. Ok

Ballast system. Ok

Hydraulic system. Ok.

Seawater. Ok.

Fresh water. Ok

High pressure air. Ok

Low pressure air.

Low pressure air. That was it. Low pressure air. Bert, in his panic at the Captain's reprimand had forgotten to isolate the sinks and toilets in the wardroom. Oh no. What should I do? I wouldn't have time to get through the crowd and shut them off myself.

In desperation I made a ship wide broadcast.

"MEM Jameson, Control Room at the rush."

No response.

I picked up the telephone and dialed the mess. Bert wasn't there. Where would he be? That was it. The hull valve and blow control was in a small compartment under the bunk spaces and there was a phone there. If I rang that, and left it ringing, Bert would answer it when he got there to do the dirty deed.

As I lifted the phone there was a strange hissing noise, followed by a rumbling and a few squeaks and squeals. I looked at the gauges for the air system. Air was being used somewhere on the boat and the pressure was dropping. The only person who could be using air was Bert. He had started to pressurize the tank.

The rumblings and squeals grew in volume. Conversation started to die down as the guests became aware of the increasing noise. Several were looking round to see where it was coming from. I knew exactly where it was coming from, and I knew exactly where it was going to. With a final whoosh, the entire contents of the sewage tank flew from the various toilets and sinks around the wardroom bathrooms, pantry and washroom. Six hundred gallons of particularly pungent human effluent burst from the tank and into the midst of the cocktail party. Turds ricocheted and splattered everywhere. Screams echoed around the control room as people desperately tried to get away from the flying filth. Too late. With a hiss, the liquid outburst ended and the remaining air in the tank began to vent, adding to the already disgraceful aroma in the area. I grabbed the microphone.

"Bert, for God's sake stop the blow." I screamed into it.

The hiss slowly faded as the pressure in the tank and the atmosphere slowly equalized. I looked around at the devastation. Most of the guest and officers had brown polka dotted clothing. Instead of cherries, everyone's drink now had a cocktail turd in it. Raw sewage was dripping from the deckhead and running down the bulkhead. The cocktail party was ruined. I sat back at the panel, my head in my hands. I was trying to look as though I was upset. In fact I was desperately biting the inside of my cheek, trying not to laugh. I could taste blood in my mouth. I heard movement in Chimney Corner and Bert peered round the corner.

"Why did you want me to stop the…"

His eyes were like saucers. His jaw had slackened.

"Shit." He exclaimed.

"Precisely Bert, and lots of it too." I replied.

The resultant aftermath took days to clear. The dry cleaning bills alone must have cost the Navy a fortune. The letters of apology were flowing for months afterwards and the Mayoral Chain had to be sent to a specialist cleaner. And Bert. Well Bert spent every minute of the remainder of our visit to Torbay cleaning shit off the wardroom walls. He was not the Captain's favourite rating, and the fine imposed at the Captain's Defaulters crippled Bert financially for several months. He was not allowed ashore for several weeks and, if the Captain had been allowed to do so, I honestly believe that he would have awarded him lashes as well. Luckily, the cat o' nine tails has been discarded as a form of naval punishment.

CHAPTER SEVENTEEN

The remainder of our visit to Torbay passed without incident. Nobody dared to misbehave after Bert's little episode. The Captain was in no mood to be trifled with and discipline aboard the boat was at an all time high.

I was studying hard for my leading hand's qualification, which would mean promotion, more money, and the wherewithal to get married. I was constantly studying, writing letters to Caroline and working.

We returned to Faslane for a well-deserved period of rest and recuperation. The boat was due to be alongside for six weeks and the crew were to take their leave during that time. I had already arranged to stay with Ray and Paula and spend some time with Caroline. I also wanted to go home and see my parents. I hadn't seen them for almost a year.

My leave was equally divided between Bedford, where my parents lived, and Aldershot, where I could spend time with Caroline. The time was rushing by and our wedding was fast approaching. I was having nothing much to do with the arrangements as I was away a great deal of the time. Caroline and her mum had booked the church, the reception, the caterers and even the honeymoon. The only thing I had booked was my leave. After all, the least I could do was turn up on the relevant date.

I managed to spend seven days with Caroline. Seven of the ten that we actually managed to see each other during the year of our engagement.

The boat's routine was, for the most part, fairly dull and routine. Patrol, back to Faslane, out on patrol again. One piece of good news was that the boat was overdue a refit. After six or seven years of being in commission and plodding around the oceans of the world, a nuclear submarine is refitted. It is put into the hands of one of the Royal Dockyards, handed over and, for the next two years, virtually stripped down to the bare hull and rebuilt.

We had been informed that Courageous was to begin refit in late September and that the work would be carried out in Chatham Dockyard. I was to be married two weeks after the refit began and, whereas the majority of the crew would be sent to other submarines, I along with a few others, would remain onboard as a skeleton crew. That meant that, all things being equal, Caroline and I could spend the first two years of married life together.

I had phoned the married quarters office in Chatham and had arranged for a house to be made available to Caroline and I once we were married. Everything seemed to be working out. Yeah, and the Pope's a protestant.

Before the refit we were allowed another couple of runs ashore. We were being sent to Hull and Liverpool. Great. All the other nuclear boats had been sent to the West Indies, Hawaii and other exotic locations. Not us. Bloody Liverpool. The crew were not impressed. Not only were we being sent to Liverpool, there was a catch, even to that. It was soon to be the seventy fifth anniversary of the Submarine

Service, and Courageous had been selected to take part in the celebrations. The crew would be paraded, in their best suits, through the centre of Liverpool, marching with rifles and bayonets. The navy certainly knew how to rub salt into the wounds.

My leave over, I headed back to Faslane and Courageous. I had enjoyed my time away from the boat and was not looking forward to the forthcoming trip. We had a three week patrol to complete before arriving at Liverpool and the mood onboard, throughout the twenty one days was, let's say, miserable. There were a number of petty squabbles and fights. The slightest thing would irritate and niggle and morale was at an all time low. The crew felt that they had been kicked in the teeth. For the two years I had now been onboard, the crew had worked hard and played hard. They had carried out every task the Navy had asked of them, and more. The morale had been good and discipline, with the odd exception, had not been a problem. The least we could have expected was a decent run ashore before the refit.

We sailed slowly up The Mersey, Liverpool to our left, Birkenhead to our right. The weather matched the crew's state of mind, miserable, and the river joined in, looking dark and dirty. The tugs, one on either side, waiting to help us through the large lock in to Queen Elizabeth Dock, were filthy dirty and ill kempt. It was drizzling and a cold wind blew across the river.

We were guided to our berth and tied up. The normal pandemonium below, with men dashing to get ashore and taste the local colour, was missing. Nobody seemed to want to leave the boat. It looked as though this was to be the worst run ashore in the history of the Submarine Service.

Eventually, leave was granted and, almost reluctantly, the crew began to filter ashore on the lookout for somewhere to stay. The dock workers were less than welcoming. Not even a wave or a greeting of any kind. I shared a taxi with a few of the crew and we made our way into the centre of Liverpool. We managed to book some rooms in the Feathers Hotel and, having dumped our bags, we retired to the nearest pub for a few beers. Some of the lads were even talking of going home for the duration of the visit, returning the night before we sailed, but that was out of the question due to the march through the city, which fell exactly halfway through the seven days we were there.

A programme of events had been published on the boat. Several trips had been arranged for the crew to local places of interest. The obligatory brewery trip was on the list, as was a guided tour of Anfield, Liverpool Football Club's Stadium. At least it would be something to do.

We began to chat with some locals in the pub. They seemed friendly enough. They invited us to clubs and pubs around the city. We invited them to have a look around the boat. Things began to take a turn for the better. Perhaps this wouldn't be too bad after all.

Submarine crews seem to have an uncanny knack of finding one pub, wherever they go, that sells cheap beer, locks the doors before the customers leave at closing time and doesn't mind a bit of rowdiness, within reason. We found one. The word was spread around the hotels and guesthouses and, later that evening, virtually the whole crew turned up at a small pub, just outside the city centre. The landlord was standing behind the bar rubbing his hands at the thought of all that money traveling from sailor's pockets into his till.

The evening began quietly enough, a bit of singing and a bit of banter with the locals. A few beers later and the fun began in earnest. One of the stokers decided that the dance of the flaming arseholes was called for. This is generally carried out to the background chanting of drunken sailors, shouting encouragement, as the star performer strips off his clothes and, as a finale, jams a rolled up newspaper between his buttocks and sets light to it before dancing round on a convenient table, while the remainder of the crew throw beer over him, trying to put out the flames. Our performer for the night was not the brightest of individuals and, having been unable to find a newspaper anywhere on the premises, had been to the gent's toilet. There he had removed a complete roll of toilet tissue, the shiny kind that looks like tracing paper, and is about as much use when it comes to wiping your arse.

He cavorted on the table in the centre of the pub, his clothes being shed and thrown around the bar. Eventually he was naked and came to the crescendo of his act. He had stripped the toilet paper from its cardboard roll and loosely folded it to allow it to be inserted between his buttocks. The pub was hot and sweaty and he was perspiring heavily by the time he had finished his athletic choreography around the table. He bent over, pulled the cheeks of his backside apart and firmly wedged the paper in the crack. He stood up clenching his buttocks and offered the paper to another stoker sitting at the table. A lighter was produced and the flame applied to the end of the tissue protruding from his backside. There was a whoosh and the whole roll went up in flames in a split second. They were halfway up the back of the unfortunate performer, who had very quickly sobered up somewhat. The smell of burning flesh permeated around the bar and the flames were so high that they started to singe the hair on the back of his head. Desperately he tried to extricate the burning mass from his backside but to no avail. His sweaty buttocks gripped the paper like a vice and the flames were too hot to allow him to pull the paper out by hand.

He began to run around the bar, his arse a sheet of flame, in an attempt to get away from the burning paper.

"For God's sake, someone put it out." He cried, by this time in real pain.

One of the radar operators stood up as the singed stoker ran past his table and threw his drink over him. Unfortunately it was a brandy and the resultant flambé nearly set light to the ceiling. One of the crew tore a curtain from the window of the pub and grabbed the stoker, rolling him on the ground in the material. Luckily the flames went out and there was a stunned silence as the extent of the damage was seen for the first time. The stoker's buttocks were a mixture of black charred flesh and red raw skin. The blisters spread up his back, almost to the neckline. An ambulance was called and the man taken away to hospital. He never returned to the boat. By the time his treatment was complete, the boat was in refit and he was sent elsewhere.

The following day was the visit to Anfield. I mentioned that I might be going to the barman at the hotel.

"You're joking." He said. "I've been wanting to walk on the pitch there for years but they won't allow it. I'll tell you what, you get me a bit of turf off the pitch, I'll give you ten quid for it."

I looked at him. He was serious. These Scousers were mad about their football. I wasn't that interested in the tour of Anfield but ten quid is ten quid.

I set off from the hotel with every intention of going to the football ground. Then, I met Dave Harman and a couple of other torpedomen. We got to drinking and, before I knew it, I had missed the tour. Oh well, there goes ten quid. I mentioned the barman's request to Dave.

"Ten quid for a bit of grass. They're bloody mad these scousers."

I could see him looking out of the window, across the road, a thoughtful expression on his face.

"What's the matter Dave?" I asked.

"Ten quid eh. Come with me."

We finished our beer and walked out into the street. Dave set off and I followed him until we reached a local park.

"I was with some bird in here last night and I noticed that the grass had just been cut. It's quite nice grass too. Could almost be good enough for Liverpool to play on."

He sat down on the wet grass and produced his seaman's knife from his pocket. He carefully cut a section of grass, about a foot square and an inch deep from the surface. He carefully rolled it up, put it under his arm and we walked away.

"You give that to the barman and we'll split it, a fiver each."

To this day I wonder what that barman did with the turf. He was over the moon with it.

"Next time Liverpool are on the tele, you look, just by the corner flag at the Kop End, you'll see where that bit came from." I told him. He duly handed over the ten pounds and secreted his prized turf away in his room. If he's reading this, I'm sorry for the deception, I apologise to the park keeper whose grass we really stole and, if you want it back, the barman in the Feathers has probably still got it, in a little shrine, in his room at the hotel. As for the ten quid, too late, Dave and I drank that the very same day.

The morning of the parade arrived. The kick off had been scheduled for two in the afternoon. They would never learn. The men began to arrive, in various states of intoxication, at the mustering point. We were to march through the city and on to the cathedral, where a service of commemoration was to be held.

The motley crew formed up. Rifles and bayonets had been issued to those deemed sober enough to be trusted, the remainder were fallen in behind. At the head of the procession was a sea cadet band and, leading our contingent was the Captain, followed by the officers, resplendent in full uniform and swords. The crew then formed the next section of the parade followed closely by ex submariners from around Britain and the world. The weather was dry but very cold and the thin naval uniforms were not designed to keep the occupant warm. It didn't take long for the cold to seep into the bones of those assembled.

"I'm busting for a piss already." One voice said.

"I've already been." Slurred another.

I looked round and could see one of the seamen standing in a steaming puddle with a relieved look on his face. The urine was beginning to run into the gutter.

The band struck up and off we went, trying to keep time with the irregular beat of the amateur band ahead. The sailor's swagger was very much in evidence but it had more to do with the consumption of alcohol than an extended period on a rolling ship. One of the crew began to sing along to the music.

"Nelly the cripple had only one nipple to feed the baby on, the poor little bugger had only one sucker to get his gob upon."

The Coxswain, marching alongside grinned and tried to regain order.

"Silence in the ranks." He said in a stern voice, spoilt rather by the drunken giggle, which he added to the end of the phrase.

The procession continued at the rather relaxed pace at which the Royal Navy marches. As we made our way through the town centre there was a general thinning of the ranks as sailors, already fed up with marching, began to creep away from the procession and, complete with rifle, bayonet fixed, headed into a convenient pub for some liquid refreshment. They were throwing the beer back as fast as they could and then jogging to catch up to the tail end. As soon as one rejoined another left. The rotational system seemed to work quite well really. As we approached the cathedral there was a slight quickening of the pace. The band was almost being pushed up the final furlong. Behind them were one hundred and ten submariners of whom at least fifty percent were drunk and most of who were breaking their necks for a pee.

"Paraaaade…Halt!"

The contingent shuffled to a halt outside the cathedral doors and before the Captain could even give the order to dismiss and for the crew to make their way inside the church for the service, there was a breaking of ranks as men disappeared to all convenient corners to relieve their aching bladders.

The service was the normal boring two hours, the monotony punctuated only by the sound of various members of the crew peeing under the pews, belching, farting and even vomiting into their caps. The farts were superb, they echoed around the church to the obvious delight of the farter and the disgust of the assembled clergy. We'd teach the navy to give us a crap run ashore.

CHAPTER EIGHTEEN

The Liverpool visit was over and it was back to Faslane to pay the boat off. We arrived alongside in the early morning and were immediately inundated with strangers crawling all over the boat to assess the work that would have to be done during the two years we would be in the refit yard at Chatham. I was called to the wardroom almost as soon as we had tied up and went in to find the Torpedo Officer, the Electrical Officer and the Torpedo Instructor sitting at a table.

"Cooke, you have been studying for your leading hands exam. It's time for you to take it. Here's the written paper. Take it into the Captain's cabin and start writing. You have two hours to complete the paper." Said the Electrical Officer.

I looked at Ben, the TI. I was stunned. I had believed that I would do the exam once we had arrived and settled down in Chatham.

"Chas, you can do this standing on your head, and if you want to get married next month, you could do with the extra pay." Said Ben.

I took the paper and walked, dazed, into the Captain's small cabin. I sat at his desk and opened the exam. I read through it. Ben was right, I knew the answers. I began to write and, instead of the two hours allowed, I completed the exam in forty five minutes. I knocked on the wardroom door and was beckoned in by the Electrical Officer. He took the offered paper from my hand and began to mark it.

"Go and get yourself a cup of tea while we mark this." He said. "We'll call you back when we're done."

I went below to the junior rates mess and poured myself a cuppa from the pot on the table. I began to have doubts about the answers I had given in the paper. Had I finished too quickly, had I rushed it and made stupid mistakes. My career, and my marriage, relied on me getting this right.

After what seemed an age I was summoned back to the wardroom where the three were still sitting, my paper on the desk in front of them.

"Sit down Cooke." Said the Torpedo Officer, who was flanked by the Electrical Officer and the TI, Ben. He pointed to a chair on the other side of the table.

"Right then Chas." It was Ben talking now. "What are the loading checks that need to be carried out on a Mark 8 mod 4 torpedo?"

I ran through the checks in my mind and then related them to the panel. There was much scribbling on bits of paper set out in front of them.

What is a SNAFU panel?" asked the Torpedo Officer.

"It's a supply null and flood unit sir, it monitors the electrical supply to the weapons via the A-link and notifies, by way of an alarm, if the supply is interrupted or shorted due to a flood in the weapon or cable."

"What is the output of the main turbo generators on the boat and what conversion machinery do we have onboard to supply alternative power? Give me three examples of what that converted power is used for." Asked the Electrical Officer.

"Describe the function and location of the water ram firing system and the purpose of the WRT Tanks."

"Detail the procedure for loading a mark 24 Tigerfish torpedo into a centre tube."

"Run through the firing procedure for a red grenade from the forward submerged signal ejector and the measures to be taken in the event of an inadvertent discharge of that grenade in the torpedo compartment during loading."

"Describe the functions of the count clock in the Mk 5 submarine laid mine and detail for me the rules, under the Geneva Convention, relating to suicide devices in mine warfare."

The questions went on and on, fired at me by all three, one after the other. My mind was in a spin but I seemed to know the answers. After about an hour the three men on the other side of the table sat back. One of the stewards was summoned and four cups of coffee were brought in.

"Well Cooke," the Electrical Officer began, "we have marked your written paper and we have tested your knowledge in an oral exam. I have the written reports from both the Torpedo Instructor and the Torpedo Officer in front of me. Their reports highly recommend you for promotion to leading hand as soon as you have passed the requisite exams. Today you have done so. You are still too young to be confirmed in the rating of leading hand but, and I'm sure the TI and Torps will agree, we intend to recommend that you be rated to Acting Leading Ordnance Electrical Mechanic as soon as is possible."

I looked at him dumbstruck. I thought I understood what he was saying but, after the mornings proceedings so far, I just wasn't sure.

"I'm sorry sir," I said, "Can you just explain that to me please?"

Ben the TI looked up. He was smiling.

"Chas, you thick git, you are going to be a leading hand as soon as the Captain can be persuaded to hold a requestman's table."

I smiled at the panel.

"Thank you very much."

The Torpedo Officer stood up and held out his hand. I took it and he shook my hand firmly.

"Well done, Chas. Go get married, and take care of her with the extra money."

I walked from the wardroom, still dazed by the speed of events.

The word soon got round the boat and everyone I saw congratulated me. I finished my work for the day and dashed to the mess in the barracks to find a phone. I was bursting to tell Caroline. We had all the arrangements in place for the wedding, we had a married quarter and now, I had the promotion. We were both over the moon. I was on my way up the ladder of success.

Two days later and I was dressed in clean working uniform with a scrubbed hat, standing outside the wardroom.

"Ordnance Electrical Mechanic Cooke." Called the Coxswain.

"Sir." I shouted and entered the room. There was a tall lectern in the centre of the room behind which stood the Captain. The Coxswain continued in the time honoured naval tradition.

"Ordnance Electrical Mechanic Cooke Sir, request to be rated to Acting Leading Electrical Mechanic."

The Captain looked to my left where the Torpedo Officer stood. He was my divisional officer and would be required to persuade the Captain that I was worthy of promotion. He went into a long diatribe and, at the end of it, I felt like looking round to see if the sun really was shining out of my arse. I couldn't believe he was talking about me. Was I that good?

The Captain peered at me over the lectern on which he was leaning.

"Well Cooke, I have heard what your divisional officer has had to say and I have read the reports on your progress since joining Courageous. I have no hesitation in rating you as Leading Electrical Mechanic. Congratulations."

I saluted and was marched out. That was it. I was now a leading hand. I took off my cap and walked away, through the control room and down to the torpedo room at the front of the boat on the deck below. As I walked in, ducking through the low doorway, Ben was sitting in his normal place on the step, doing some paperwork. I walked past him and put my cap on my bunk.

"Do you fancy a cup of tea Ben?" I asked.

He looked at me.

"Not from you, not while you are in that disgusting state." He said.

I was gob smacked. I was wearing clean shirt and trousers, my boots had been polished and I had even had my hair trimmed.

"You are incorrectly dressed and out of the rig of the day. I will allow you to make me a cup of tea when, and only when, you have corrected your uniform."

"Sorry Ben, I don't understand."

"What is your rank or rating?" Ben enquired.

"Well, as of about three minutes ago, I'm a leading hand."

"Exactly, you are a leading hand and yet you do not have the required badges of rank on your arm. You are therefore incorrectly dressed." He grinned and threw me a badge. It was a blue fouled anchor on a white background. A needle and cotton were pushed through the badge.

"I'll tell you what Chas. You sit there and sew that on and I'll make you a cup of tea." He stood up, patted me on the shoulder, grinned and went off to make the tea. He was, despite his frightening exterior, a bit of a softy, and he took a real care and pride over, what he saw as, his boys, the torpedomen.

My new promotion was a real bonus. I was immediately slightly better off financially and a leading hand in the Royal Navy is equivalent to a Corporal in the army, so I was treated a little more like an adult. Although, unlike the army, the leading hands in the Navy do not have their own mess, and there are no social privileges to go with the promotion, it was the first step on the ladder. Unfortunately, it would also, later on, mean a return to HMS Collingwood for a six month qualifying course. But for now, I was looking forward to the refit in Chatham, marriage and some time ashore with my wife to be.

The trip to Chatham was coming up and, almost as soon as the boat arrived there I would be going on leave and getting married. There was the small problem of having my banns read first though. I went to see the padre in the barracks and, because I was unable to be a regular parishioner at any church, my banns consisted of a notice to be pinned on the ship's notice-board. I tucked the form away in my locker until the day I was due to go on leave and then handed the completed form to Cliff, my best man to be.

"Here, Cliff, I don't want the lads to have the opportunity to take the piss over this so, when I go on leave tomorrow, just pin this on the notice board and I'll take it down when I get back, okay?"

"Not a problem Chas." Said Cliff, looking at the form I had given him.

The boat, by now, was in Chatham, tied up alongside the jetty, waiting to go into the dry dock. We had been living in HMS Pembroke, the naval barracks at Chatham. The accommodation for refit crews was normally very good but, for some reason, we had been stuck in a Napoleonic wars vintage messdeck in which forty men slept on metal bunk beds and shared a single toilet and shower, which was a five minute walk along the freezing cold pavements. I was glad to be getting out of the place.

My last duty before I left to get married was to play rugby for the boat against the crew of the submarine just completing its refit, HMS Churchill. Just as I was about to leave for the match I received a telephone call from the married quarters office, ordering me to go and see the officer in charge. I just had time to nip up there and see him before the match.

"Ah, Cooke, come in." said the young lieutenant.

"I gather there are some papers to be signed sir." I said, reaching for my pen.

"Not exactly. There's been a slight hitch I'm afraid. It's your married quarter you see."

"What do you mean a slight hitch sir?" I asked.

"Well Cooke, one of the crew from the Hong Kong Squadron has had to come back to the UK. Now obviously, we can't expect him to commute to Kowloon each day so I'm afraid he's been given your married quarter."

"Okay sir, he's got mine, where am I going to have a quarter then?" I asked, unprepared for the bombshell about to follow.

"That's just it you see, we don't have any more married quarters, you haven't got one to move into."

"So what the heck am I supposed to do then?" I exploded. I could just imagine Caroline's face when I told her we were homeless before we were even married.

"There's nothing I can do Cooke, we have nowhere left. You'll just have to postpone your marriage I'm afraid."

"You are sodding joking I hope, I'm getting married the day after tomorrow and now you decide to tell me I haven't got a house to live in. That's shit and you know it is." I shouted. A young sailor looked round the door to see what the noise was all about. I glared at him. "And you can get your face out of the door too mate."

He decided that he suddenly had some very important business elsewhere and ran out of the married quarter's office and headed toward the NAAFI. The last thing he wanted was to witness some dirty submariner punching an officer and then have to give evidence at a court martial.

The young officer just sat there and looked at the papers on his desk. I turned on my heel and stormed out, slamming the door so hard on the way out that I heard the portrait of the Queen hit the floor as it was shaken from the wall where it had previously hung. Oh bollocks. I had thirty six hours to find somewhere to live or Caroline and I would be returning from our honeymoon and going to separate addresses.

I walked to the sports pitches and I was in just the mood for rugby. It was an excuse to legally take out my aggression on some unfortunate bloke from the opposition. I got changed in silence and made my way out onto the pitch. I looked around the field and picked out the biggest bloke I could see in the other half of the pitch. There he was, a gorilla in a rugby shirt. I was going to have him as soon as I could get near him. The whistle blew and the ball sailed through the air from the centre spot toward me. I caught it cleanly and was immediately splattered into the ground by a horde of hairy arsed sailors dressed as rugby players. A ruck formed over me and then I felt a searing pain in my left leg. I was screaming and as the ruck broke up and play moved off I was left flat on the mud. I looked at my leg and was amazed to see that the sock had been torn off of the calf and the side of my leg was already twice its normal size and black, not with mud, but with blood under the skin. Some bastard had stamped on me about four times. I couldn't move my leg. Oh great, that was all I needed, no house, no feeling in my leg and, unless I was fixed very quickly, no bloody wedding. I was going to be the flavour of the month with Caroline and her family now.

I was carried from the field on a stretcher and taken to the sick bay in the barracks where my leg was x-rayed. Luckily there were no broken bones and the injury was diagnosed as a torn muscle and severe bruising. It was three hours later that I hobbled from the sick bay, my leg swathed in bandages, and limped my way to Chatham railway station to start my leave. I still had the problem of finding somewhere to live, and quick.

I made a number of frantic phone calls while waiting for my train and, eventually, my Aunt, who lived in Northfleet, offered to take us in until we were given a married quarter. I broke the news to Caroline, who was brilliant about the whole thing and assured me that, as long as we were together, she didn't mind where we lived. I breathed a sigh of relief.

The day before our wedding I had been invited to stay with Brian, Caroline's brother, and his family, in Guildford. I had met Brian several times and we seemed to hit it off fairly well. Caroline's elder brother, John, would also be staying at the house. I turned up, bag in hand and my wedding suit over my arm and settled in.

That evening, to calm my nerves, Brian and John took me to the local pub. For once I was sensible. I had very little to drink. The least I could do for Caroline was turn up on time and sober for the wedding. I went to bed that night, surprised that I didn't feel nervous. I was really looking forward to marrying Caroline.

I awoke with a start. It was still almost dark. I looked at the clock next to the bed and saw that it was still only five thirty. Unable to sleep, I washed and dressed and went downstairs for a cigarette only to find that the packet was empty. I decided to go to the local newsagent, just five minutes walk down the road, and was just about to leave via the front door when I had a thought. I didn't have a key and if I shut the door behind me I would be unable to get back in. Easy, go out the back door and take the key from the lock, lock the door behind me, then I would be able to return without having to wake any of the sleeping family. I carefully and quietly shut and locked the door behind me and made my way down the back garden path to the gate. It was padlocked and there was no key. Never mind. I was a fairly athletic kind of guy, I could climb over the fence. I scaled the slippery wooden fence panels and was astride the top when I began to giggle. The giggle turned into laughter. Here I was, at six o'clock on the morning of my wedding, climbing over the back fence of my future brother in law's house. If he looked out of the window now he would think I was legging it and leaving his sister in the lurch. For some reason I found that highly amusing. I soon stopped laughing when I realised that Brian and John would probably beat the living daylights out of me if they saw me. Quickly I dropped down the other side and ran off to get my cigarettes. Luckily the two brothers had drunk a little more than me and never woke up. I managed to return without incident.

The rest of the morning went by in a blur and I was soon getting ready for the wedding. First crisis of the day: I had bought a pair of mid calf length boots to go with my suit and, because of the bandages on my leg, the left boot wouldn't go on. I had to cut the leather to make them fit, ruining the boots. I turned up at the church with my best man, Cliff, who had decide to wear full naval uniform which, I thought, was a little foolhardy considering that I was getting married in Aldershot and that the town was inhabited by about thirty thousand soldiers. Standing outside the church I recall that Cliff was a nervous wreck and that I spent the entire time telling him jokes and trying to calm him down. Surely this was the wrong way round.

Caroline turned up bang on time. She looked beautiful. It was a full white wedding with all the bells and whistles. She and her mother had planned it superbly and the whole service went perfectly. Toward the end, Caroline and I were called forward to the altar rail where the vicar beckoned to us to kneel for the blessing. Crisis two. My leg, swathed in bandages, wouldn't bend. I had to be helped down by Caroline and I must have looked like a lame donkey with my left leg stuck straight out to the rear. As I knelt, there was a fit of giggling from the congregation behind. I couldn't figure out what they found so amusing. It was only later that I found out that my brother Ray had somehow managed to sabotage my boots. On the sole of the left foot he had written H E, and on the right, L P. Caroline and I were the only two people in the church who were unable to see my involuntary cry for assistance.

The reception went on into the late evening and, eventually, Caroline and I left for our honeymoon. Again, I had been unable to help with the planning and Caroline and her mum had made all the arrangements. Our wedding night was to be spent at the Hog's Back Hotel, between Aldershot and Guildford, before we travelled to Cornwall the following day for the remainder of our honeymoon. I do remember that we were both so knackered that, I suspect, like many other newly weds, we went to bed and fell asleep.

The following day we made our way to the railway station and set off for Looe in Cornwall. It was a long journey and, at seven o'clock that evening we arrived in Liskeard to change trains for the final short leg of the trip. I settled Caroline down, with our luggage, on a platform bench, and set off to find out the time of the next train to Looe. I found the only member of staff working and made the enquiry.

"The next train to Looe." He said, pulling a tattered timetable from his jacket pocket. "That will be at seven fifty three."

I looked at my watch, seven twenty seven.

"Oh great, only half an hour or so to wait then, thank you." I said, and began to walk off.

"Tomorrow morning." He added.

I stopped dead in my tracks and looked at him. He wasn't joking.

"Is there somewhere we can get a taxi then?" I asked the man.

"Taxi? There's only one taxi works here on a Sunday and that's Fred. He's not here. He took a fare somewhere a little while ago. He could be hours yet."

I explained to the man that Caroline and I had just got married and he softened.

"I tell you what my dear," he said in that deep Cornish accent, "You step across the road to the pub and have something to eat and drink, and, as soon as he comes back I'll get Fred to come and fetch you."

I thanked him and, following his directions, Caroline and I left the station and went to the local hostelry where we sat down to a drink and a hot pasty.

About an hour later the door opened and an elderly gent, obviously the worse for wear and with a bright red, drinker's nose, staggered through the door and made his way to the bar. Caroline and I chuckled at him, he could hardly stand up. He spoke to the landlord who banged his fist on the counter several times until the bar became silent.

"Taxi for Mr and Mrs Cooke." He called.

I held up my hand and the landlord saw me. He directed the drunken man to my table. Oh God, he was our taxi driver. We followed him to a wreck of a car outside the pub and settled into the back seat. In the front passenger seat was a woman who, to this day, I can only assume, was Fred's wife. She was also drunk. Off we went. Fred seemed to drive everywhere at one hundred miles an hour, using the white line in the centre of the road as a rough guide to where the car should be going. His wife just sat in the front leering at Caroline and I, hiccupping loudly. The country roads presented a challenge to Fred. They were narrow and winding but, that white line down the centre kept him roughly on course. The journey was punctuated by the occasional glare of headlights as we met oncoming cars. Fred hogged the white line until the last minute and then swerved out of the way, to one side or the other, it didn't seem to matter to Fred which side, and then, as soon as the car had passed, horn blaring, he threw the car back to the comfort of the white line.

Eventually, with Caroline and I petrified and shaking, we drew up outside the Rock Towers Hotel in Looe. Fred, who must have been eighty at least, insisted on carrying our bags up the steep slope to the door before charging me the princely sum of one pound for the trip. I doubled his money with an equal tip and, glad to be alive, Caroline and I made our way into the hotel.

We had phoned from the pub to let the staff know we would be late and they had saved us a meal. It was obvious that Caroline or her mum had let slip that it was our honeymoon. The three women on duty spent the whole meal fussing over us, smiling and cooing. They were very kind but Caroline and I just wanted to have some peace and quiet.

After the meal, we went back to reception where we collected our key.

"Now then my dears, we have put your bags in your room, here's your key. You'll have to be a bit careful because the door locks are a bit strange. You have to turn the key three times to open it and three times to lock it. Security locks, you know."

I thanked the lady, and we headed off to our room on the first floor. I put the key in the lock and, remembering the instructions, began to turn the key. It was a bit stiff. I turned a little harder and, reluctantly the key began to turn. I had managed one complete revolution when I realised that, although the key was turning, the lock wasn't. I withdrew it from the door and looked at it. It was grossly malformed, the key now looking like a pig's tail with a lovely spiral twist in it.

I returned to reception where I presented the key to the male owner of the hotel. He looked at me.

"Oh dear, that's the only key we have for your room." He said with a sad look. "I'll have to try and straighten it out for you now." And with that he disappeared into the kitchen. I waited at reception and, suddenly, I was startled by a loud banging. Caroline came dashing down the stairs to see what was going on and we both peered through the partially open kitchen door. We could see the hotel owner inside. He had our room key, firmly grasped in a pair of large pliers, over a high flame on the gas cooker and was pounding it back into shape with what appeared to be a large hammer. Caroline and I looked at each other and laughed. What a start to married life.

Eventually the key was straightened, some oil applied to the door lock and we were able, finally, to get into our room. We fell on the bed exhausted. It was quite a nice room but strangely laid out. The bathroom was through a door in the wall at the bottom of the bed and ran the width of the room. It was particularly narrow. The bath was against one wall and there was just enough room between it and the opposite wall to walk, sideways, along its length to the tap end. The toilet was at the other end of the bathroom and would allow anyone seated upon it just enough room to get their knees between the toilet itself and the opposite wall. We fell into bed, determined to have our wedding night, even though it was twenty four hours late. Above the head of the bed was a set of controls for the radio, alarm clock, lights and an intercom to reception for room service. I managed to fiddle with all the switches and found some romantic music on the radio and we settled down for a romantic night. Finally we fell asleep exhausted.

I was awoken the next morning by a strange buzzing noise. I slowly came round and realised that it was coming from the panel above the bed. I must have accidentally set the alarm clock while I was tuning the radio and playing with the lights. I looked at the clock, it was six thirty. I pressed various buttons at random while Caroline looked on, still half asleep. Eventually the noise stopped and I was turning over to go back to sleep when a voice came out of the speaker above my head.

"Good morning Mr and Mrs Cooke. Will you be taking breakfast this morning?"

I looked at Caroline who, sleepily, shook her head. I searched the control panel and found the button marked 'Intercom'.

"No, thank you." I said into the panel.

"In that case Mr Cooke, perhaps you could turn off the intercom. It's been on all night you see."

I again looked at Caroline who was pulling the blankets over her head. I could see her face was a deep shade of red.

"Thank you." I said, and turned off the offending intercom. Oh God, what else could go wrong?

I was in urgent need of relief. I got out of bed and, naked, staggered, still half asleep into the bathroom. It's always a delicate moment for a newly wed. Do you leave the door open or do you shut it and lock it. I took the middle of the road sort of decision. I went into the bathroom and shut the door but left it unlocked. I sat on the throne to evacuate my bowels, as they would say in hospital. In the navy it was more colourfully known as strangling your morning George or emptying ones dung locker. Whatever you want to call it, I did it. I had been sitting there contemplating the start to our married life for a few minutes when a noise brought me back to full consciousness. I could hear people talking, and they weren't far away. I looked to my left and realised that I was sitting on a toilet which had been strategically placed next to a full length, floor to ceiling window, and, what was more, it was clear and not frosted glass and the curtains were still wide open. Below me I could see the early risers taking their morning promenade on the seafront below. What was worse, they could see me just as clearly. One elderly lady even smiled and waved. I actually bloody waved back. I threw the curtains across the window and decided that somebody had it in for me. What had I done to deserve this. What was more, if this was my kind of luck, what had Caroline done to deserve me. I went back into the bedroom and warned Caroline about the window. If I had expected any kind of sympathy from my new wife I was very much mistaken, she nearly wet herself laughing.

Luckily, there were no more serious mishaps on our honeymoon. For October the weather was wonderful and we came towards the end of our first week together, happy, but, with the prospect of moving into a small bedroom in my Aunt's house, we weren't looking forward to leaving Looe.

CHAPTER NINETEEN

The honeymoon over we made our way back to Kent and a single bed in a small bedroom in my aunt's first floor maisonette. It was hardly what I had planned. All newly weds have the dream of settling into a home of their own, roses round the porch and all that. We had a view of the muddy River Thames just the other side of the cement works. It was our home for three months and it was no fun for any of us. My aunt was great but the house was crowded with four adults and two children living in the three bedroomed house. Caroline was at home all day and I had to leave at five in the morning and didn't get home till about seven each evening. But, for all the problems, Caroline and I made the most of it and were happy to be together.

Eventually the navy decided, after much harassment from me, to find a house for us. There were still no married quarters available so a private house was rented and handed over to Caroline and I. It was lovely, a three bedroomed bungalow in the middle of the Kent orchards about six miles from Chatham. It was two miles from the nearest bus stop or shops but we didn't mind, we were alone at last.

Being a non driver, getting to work entailed a two mile walk, a five mile bus ride and another mile walk at the other end. The only bus that I could catch left at six am so I had to get up at four thirty every morning. The only bus home was at six so I finally arrived each evening at about seven thirty. It was a long day but I had the prospect of our own home to come back to at the end of the long day of hard and often dirty work at the base.

Even though the submarine was in refit I still had to be part of the duty watch every fourth day and that meant staying in the base overnight and leaving Caroline alone at home. But we managed and we were, for the most part, really happy.

We had been in the house for about three months and we thought that our trials were over. Oh you foolish things. How naïve could we be?

"LOEM Cooke, report to the coxswains office".
The tannoy in the mess room broke my concentration and I put down my cup of coffee, made the short walk along the passageway to the relevant office and knocked on the door.
"Ah, Chas, come in, I've got something for you".
"What's that then Cox'n?"
"A draft chit, you're leaving us in two weeks."
I took the slip of paper from his hand and, with a sinking heart, read the printed instructions. I was to join HMS Collingwood, back in Fareham, to start my Leading Hands Professional Qualifying Course. It was exactly twenty five weeks long. One week short of the six months required to allow me to move Caroline to Portsmouth with me. That meant that, once again, we would be separated. I would only be able to get home at the weekend, assuming that I wasn't duty watch. Great, how was I going to break this to Caroline. Once again, just as the world seemed to be getting a little rosier for us, someone in the drafting office had heard the 'Chas is Happy' alarm and decided to do something about it. I'm sure they had it in for me.

Again Caroline amazed me. She seemed to be able to take these things on the chin. She accepted the news as just another problem to be overcome. I loved her more and more every time something like this happened. I knew I had made the right choice when I had asked Caroline to marry me.

Two weeks later, and still suffering from the hangover caused by my leaving run, I left Courageous and headed off to Portsmouth, leaving Caroline alone and, by this time in the early stages of pregnancy, I caught the train and headed off toward Portsmouth and another six months away from home. I knew that the course would enable me to get on in the navy and work toward my next advancement up the ladder but I was a relative newly wed and I wanted to be with my wife. Still, no good griping and dripping, best get on with it.

I arrived back at HMS Collingwood and was given my accommodation. At least it was better than the last time I had been here. Now it was a four man messdeck in a fairly new block. As I was on a course I had a fairly relaxed routine of tuition during the day, and evenings to myself. I was required to form part of the duty watch once every four days but, as a leading hand I had little to do other than supervise the new recruit trainees who actually did the donkey work. Every Wednesday afternoon was a sports make and mend and we could choose any sport we wanted to. I hated running but loved football so, that was what I did. Learnt about electrical and hydraulic systems, played football and, as long as I wasn't duty watch, I went home at the weekends. I was actually managing to get home about every other weekend. I had found another bloke who lived in Chatham and who drove home every weekend and I got a lift with him and paid him petrol money. Things weren't as bad as I had thought they would be.

About four months into the course, on a Monday morning the sports list came round as usual. You had to select which sport you wanted to do each Wednesday so that they could check you went and made sure you didn't leg it into the nearest pub for the afternoon. I looked forward to the football each week and as the list was passed to me I had my pen poised. Smudge Smith passed me the paper with a look of disgust. I cast my eyes over it only to see that it was a notice rather than a list.

'Inter Departmental Cross Country.' It said. 'All ratings under training will take part in the inter departmental cross-country competition this Wednesday afternoon. The race will take place over a six mile course in the local area and will be strictly stewarded by the Physical Training Staff. All to take part. No absences accepted without the signed permission of a course supervising officer or medical certificate. All ratings to muster on the parade ground at 1400 hours, prompt. Absentees will be disciplined.'

I looked at Smudge who, like me, was a lazy, twenty ciggies a day, four pints a night man. I didn't do running, it was against my religion. Smudge looked devastated, as though he had experienced a death in the family.

"Good God, Chas. They can't be serious can they?" He asked with a look of desperation.

"I think they are mate." I said.

"Cooke, Smith, do you have a problem that we need to know about?" I looked up. It was the Chief Petty Officer instructor speaking.

"No Chief, just discussing the advantages of transistors over valves in electrical equipment." I said.

"Bollocks. Pay attention and leave your chatter till lunch."

"Yes Chief. Sorry Chief."

I returned to my books and tried to concentrate on the lesson. At last lunch came along and Smudge and I spent the entire break trying to come up with some way of getting out of the cross country. You would have thought that the combined brain power of two naval technical ratings could have come up with something, but no. It looked as though we were going to have to bite the bullet and run.

I spent the following thirty six hours trying to find an excuse not to run. I reported to the sick bay and complained of everything from piles to yellow swamp fever. The morning sick bay clinic was packed with men trying to find an illness which would allow them to miss the cross country. Obviously somebody had had a word with the scablifters, I even saw one bloke coming out on crutches with the MO shouting after him.

"The exercise will do that torn ligament good. You get out there and do the run. You'll see, you'll enjoy it."

He passed me muttering.

"If it's that bleeding enjoyable why isn't he volunteering to do it then…bastard."

Come the Wednesday morning I finally began to accept the fact that I was going to have to take part. All the previous day and all that morning it had rained non-stop and now it was blowing a hooligan with sleet in the air. I was thrilled.

"Okay, that's it for the forenoon, off you go to lunch and good luck in the run this afternoon. See you all tomorrow morning." The Chief was grinning like an idiot. He didn't have to do the run. He could go home and slip into a nice warm wife. It was alright for him. He wasn't going to have a massive coronary in the middle of some bog on the outskirts of Fareham was he?

I ate very little for lunch. The more I ate the more there was for me to spew up. Just before 1400 there was a knock on the door of the mess and there stood Smudge, resplendent in his best running kit. Slowly and without much conversation we made our way to the parade ground which, at HMS Collingwood was huge, almost a quarter of a mile along each side.

We stood there having a last fag, shivering in the freezing wind while, all around us, fit, athletic looking men carried out their stretching exercises and warmed up for the race. They were very professional looking in their Adidas running shorts, Puma trainers and silky running vests.

I looked at Smudge. He was wearing a crumpled T-shirt with a picture of a large breasted, semi-naked model on the front and the slogan "Been there, shagged that" on the back. His feet were clad in a dirty pair of white pusser's plimsolls with a split down one side of the right foot and his shorts were khaki and held up by a bit of string. I didn't look much better than him either. He was smiling and I thought he must have had couple of stiff shorts before he came out.

The PT staff began calling everyone into line in preparation for the off. The course had been publicised on the notice boards in all the messdecks and it had obviously been designed by a sadistic bastard who hated sailors. A starting pistol went off and there was a huge rush toward the top of the parade ground. Smudge grabbed me by the arm.

"Just hang on and let the crowd get away, I've got a plan." He said with a grin.

At the top of the parade ground was a long straight road leading to the main entrance of the establishment and the course then took the runners across the road and onto the sports fields before meandering off for miles across the surrounding fields. We hadn't even got to the top of the parade ground and I was gasping for breath. Smudge, who was six foot one, just loped along beside me, a fag in his mouth and a stupid grin on his head. What the hell was he up to?

Eventually we reached the main gate, we were already last and my throat and lungs were burning. I could feel my face glowing and my arms and legs were bloody freezing in the chill wind. The runners in front of us reached the main gate and disappeared from view and, as we exited the gate behind them they were already across the road and nearly at the sports fields. I was suddenly spun off my feet and my shoulder nearly wrenched from its socket. I felt myself being dragged along and my hip bounced off a wall as my face hit a wooden post. I suddenly realised what the hell was going on. Just outside the main gate was an old latrine block, rarely used but still standing. Smudge had pulled me inside and was pushing the dilapidated wooden door shut behind us. He had obviously planned this for some time as he produced a long piece of four by two wood, which he used to jam the door shut. From the cistern above one of the toilets he produced two bottles of beer and from under one of the sinks he produced a pack of cards.

"There you go Chas." He said, passing me a bottle and a bottle opener. "Fill your boots mate."

He slurped from his beer and then explained the plan.

"It's easy Chas me old mate. All we do is wait here until the runners come back, then we join in. Nobody'll know we haven't run the entire course and we get to sit here, play cards and have a couple of beers while they leg it around the countryside like a bunch of lunatics. What do you reckon then, eh?"

I had to admit, I was impressed. It was a bit chilly sitting in that old latrine block but that was so much better than running a six mile cross country race.

The time passed, helped along by the odd hand of crib and the occasional beer and, eventually we heard the slip slap of wet trainers on tarmac as the lead runners began to make their way toward the finishing line. We waited until a suitable number of runners had gone past, after all, we didn't want to look like Olympic athletes, and then we prepared to join in with the field.

"Right Chas, you get rid of that bit of wood so we can get out." Said Smudge.

I turned round to move the obstruction and was hit by a freezing cold cascade of water from behind.

"What the f…!"

I turned round to see what was going on and immediately received a stinging slap to the side of my face. Smudge had gone wibbly fish. He'd become a homicidal maniac and was attacking me.

"What the hell…"

Whack. Another slap to the other side of the face. My head was reeling and my vision was blurred.

"Come on then Chas, hit me now."

I looked at Smudge who was standing there with his face thrust toward me. Water was running from his soaked hair.

"Smudge, what the bloody hell are you on, what's all this about?" I asked.

"Chas, you're really not devious enough for this game are you. If we go out there dry as a bone and fresh faced they'll know we haven't been running. The water will make it look as though you've been sweating and if we slap each others face it will make our cheeks red and we'll look hot and bothered. Now come on, hit me."

I probably went a bit over the top because by the time I'd finished Smudge looked as though he was about to lose consciousness.

"Thanks Chas." He said through streaming eyes. He licked the small droplet of blood from the corner of his mouth and moved to the door. He opened it a crack and peered out.

"Right, just wait for a little gap and then, when I say go, go."

There was a small pause and then,

"GO."

We burst out of the door. It was timed to perfection. The runner in front of us had just turned the corner out of sight and the next placed man was still nowhere to be seen.

"Shit."

"What Smudge?"

"Our plimsoles, they're not muddy, quick, rub 'em in this."

He had found a small grassy patch of mud and moss against the wall of the outbuilding and we frantically dirtied our plimsoles before jogging round the corner, gasping and panting as though we were on our last legs. As we ran through the main gate I could see, stretched out in front of us, all the way to the parade ground, a gaggle of knackered and sweating sailors who had just spent the last hour running round the local bogs and swamps. Smudge and I plodded down the main road toward the finishing area where the PT staff had erected one of those rope funnels that force you into single file to be counted as you cross the line.

Smudge and I really put on a show. We sprinted the last fifty yards or so, doing our best to beat each other to the line. Smudge just pipped me at the post as we thundered down the last few yards. We slowed to a gasping amble as we made our way through the rope funnel and gave our names to the Clubswinger. We walked slowly through the remainder of the rope path, hands on hips, gasping for breath and bent at the waist, dragging in great lungfuls of air. The fifty yard sprint had done for both of us and we didn't need to pretend now. The clubswinger who had taken our names trotted past us, looking at us as he went.

"Well done lads, bloody good effort." He said as he passed.

Smudge looked at me and grinned, we'd shown them, we'd fooled them all.

As we exited the ropes a slim athletic looking Lieutenant was watching us.

"Cooke, Smith, brilliant, absolutely brilliant. Report to me."

I was worried, had we been rumbled.

We made our way across to where he was standing. I had still some way to go before full recovery and Smudge was so far gone he had even given up trying to light his roll up.

"Yes sir." We said in unison.

"I'm bloody impressed. I look forward to next week. We'll do really well I feel." Said the officer with a grin.

"I'm sorry sir, I don't understand." I said.

Next week, HMS Cambridge." Said the Rupert raising his eyebrows.

"Sir, what are you on about?" Said Smudge.

"You two were the first home in your age group, you have achieved automatic selection for the annual cross country match against HMS Cambridge, in Plymouth, next week. It's a much tougher course than this one, plenty of hills and water. I think we'll do really well this year. I'll contact your course instructor tomorrow to arrange for you to be released for the run." He said and, with that, turned on his heel and almost skipped away back to the finish line.

I looked at Smudge. His jaw was wide open and the roll up was hanging from his bottom lip. I'm sure I could see the lip trembling. I thought he was going to cry.

"Smudge, you are an absolute ******* ****."

The next Thursday at about four pm, Smudge and I had to try and explain to the young Lieutenant.

"Forty minutes, forty minutes, how can you have been that far behind their last place man?" He asked, pleading for an explanation.

Smudge and I were covered from head to foot in mud, Smudge had spew on his running vest and I was in the middle of a racking coughing spasm as I tried to draw breath into my body.

"Sorry sir," said Smudge, "I think it was that curry they served in the Junior Rates dining room last night. We've both been up all night. We were shitting through the eye of a needle for hours."

"I think we could be dehydrated sir." I chipped in.

Again he presented us with his back and walked off shaking his head. All I could hear was him muttering "Forty bloody minutes behind, forty, bloody forty…"

It was a very lonely coach trip back to Portsmouth that night. I don't think anyone said a single word to either of us. Still, at least they never asked us to run again. Not one of our most successful dodges that one.

CHAPTER TWENTY

It was almost Christmas 1977. It was freezing and we were well into the course. The sooner I got it over and done with, the sooner I could go home to Caroline who, by now was heavily pregnant. The baby was due in only a few weeks and I still had four months to go before the course was over. Caroline and I had the prospect of having a new born baby and still being separated all week, only seeing each other at weekends. I was beginning to worry. Caroline didn't drive and our house was nearly two miles from the nearest bus stop or shop. All there was in the little bit of habitation around our home was four other houses and a pub. It was going to be difficult for Caroline after the birth.

The news at the time was full of the predicted fireman's strike over pay and conditions. Little was I to know how much it would affect me.

One day, in the middle of instruction a piece of paper was handed to the instructor who stopped what he was doing and looked up.

"Okay lads, listen up. I've got some news for you all."

A hush quickly came over the classroom as we waited for him to let us in on the secret.

"Right then gents, the fire brigade union have announced that they will be calling a national strike as from next week. The government has, God help us all, decided that the services will provide firefighting cover. All courses are suspended forthwith and tomorrow you will all be detailed for training at the Naval Firefighting School, HMS Phoenix. There you will learn all there is to know about the green goddess. And before you ask, that is a fire engine, circa world war two, of which they have held thousands in mothballs for just such a time. So, finish what you are doing and then you have the afternoon off. You will be required to attend the naval stores where all the necessary clothing and equipment is ready to be issued. Off you go."

There was a general shuffling and then a burst of shouting and calling.

"Here, Chas, I hear they always put ginger haired gits in first 'cos they burn better."

"Baggsy driving the fire engine, I've always wanted to be a fire engine driver."

"Pugh, Pugh, Barney McGrew, Cuthbert, Dibble and Grubb."

Slowly we made our way out of the classroom and back to our messes. After lunch we joined the huge queue at the naval stores where there was a mountain of combat jackets and trousers and Wellington boots. It was a free for all and no-one was counting so I managed to get two combat jackets, one for firefighting and one for 'best', as they say. It'd save me having to buy a new coat at least.

The following days were spent in grooming a bunch of matelots in the delicate art of firefighting. The green goddesses were delivered and a whole host of Heavy Goods Vehicle driving Examiners appeared at Collingwood to test the driving skills of any matelot that could drive. The test went something along the following lines.

"Okay, if you would start it up for me. Good. Now, move it forward. Thank you, now move it back to where you started from. Good. Thank you. Here's your licence. Next!"

There were people driving them I wouldn't have trusted on a bicycle, let alone an unstable, water carrying, ancient fire engine with a crash gearbox.

Next it was off to the firefighting school where, along with servicemen from the army and air force, we were put through our paces.

Now most sailors are taught the basics of firefighting any way. After all, there aren't many fire engines available in the middle of the Atlantic Ocean. The squaddies, well they were another matter altogether. I stood, one day, watching the Royal Irish Rangers rigging a green goddess to extract water from a lake and pump it, through hoses to the fire. The back end of the fire engine looked like a fisherman's bait box, a bag of worms to be precise. For twenty minutes they were running hoses here there and everywhere. Finally, in true military style, they all fell in, dressed off in perfect line and were called to attention by their corporal. One soldier was detailed off to man the pump while two others held the hose nozzle toward the flames.

"Water on." Screamed the corporal and the pump rose to a whining crescendo as it pumped five hundred gallons of water a minute out of the lake, into the back of the green goddess and then through about three hundred yards of perfectly laid out hose, straight back into the lake. Somebody had forgotten to connect the hose with the nozzle on into the loop. I nearly wet myself laughing along with about two hundred spectating matelots.

The Ghurkas were nearly as bad. They were doing breathing apparatus drills and, to test their ability to follow a guide-line through a smoke filled house, their face masks were blacked out so that they were unable to see. The instructor coaxed them in to the building and off they went, groping along, one behind the other, like a line of blinded war wounded. While the instructor's attention was on the Ghurkas some wag of a matelot took the other end of the guide line and, where it exited the building, extended it by about twenty yards directly into the lake. All twenty five of the little Nepalese fighting men groped their way straight out of the building and into the water. I tell you something, those Ghurkas do not like being laughed at by a bunch of badly dressed half pissed matelots. There was very nearly bloodshed.

It took only three days to train us all to be masters of the art of fighting fires. We were pronounced ready for action and stood by for our postings. We had been told that we were almost certain to be sent as close to our families as possible so we could go home when not required. I breathed a sigh of relief. Caroline had already gone into labour once but it had been stopped by the doctors because she was too early. It wasn't going to be long before the birth now and, to be honest, this fireman's strike couldn't have come at a better time.

"Okay, pay attention for your postings. I can tell you now, you will be going to one of only two places so listen in, you will be leaving first thing in the morning for Christmas leave and will then report to your allotted place of duty on the morning of the 29th of December at 0800.

Brown, Croydon, Davison, Croydon, Greenhalge, Croydon."

This was looking good. Croydon wasn't that far from Chatham by train. I could be home in under an hour.

The list went on and on.

"Mctavish, Croydon."

There was an anguished cry from the back of the group.

"Croydon, Croydon, but aim frae Glasgae, that's not near hame fer me."

I looked round, it would appear that Jock McTavish was not happy with his posting to Croydon then, oh well, never mind.

"Blackwood, Croydon, Wilson, Croydon, Smith P, Croydon, Smith G, Croydon, Cooke,"

Here it comes, my passport to time at home with the wife....

"Glasgow. Jackson, Glasgow...."

The list went on and on while I stood there in stunned silence. Glasgow. No, somebody was having a little leg pull at my expense. It couldn't be any farther from my pregnant wife.

I stood rooted to the spot while the remainder of the names were called out.

"Are you okay Chas?" I looked around. Everybody else had gone.

I looked up, it was the Chief Petty Officer Instructor.

"I'm going to Glasgow Chief."

"Yeah, so I heard. What's wrong with that then?"

"But my wife lives in Chatham and she's pregnant. The baby's due in a couple of weeks. Am I allowed to swap with Jock McTavish or another one that's going to Croydon?"

"Sorry Chas, they've decided that no-one can swap at such short notice, it'd cause chaos son. You'll have to go to Glasgow mate. Can't be helped, life in a blue suit I'm afraid."

I wandered back to the mess and packed my bag for leave. How much bad news could Caroline stand? It had been nothing but one kick in the groin after another since we had been married and she had took it all without any complaint. But this? Just when we really needed to be close to one another the Navy had pulled another blinder.

The following morning I took the train home to Chatham. I caught the bus from the station and walked the last two miles down the country lanes. It was freezing cold and there was snow in the air.

Caroline sensed that something was wrong as soon as I walked into our house. I broke the news and she looked up at me. There were tears in her eyes.

"Never mind love, It'll all work out okay. I'll be fine. You just make sure you look after yourself up there, do you hear me?" and with that she walked into the kitchen to make a cup of tea. She was incredible, she was so much stronger than I had realised. She was doing better than me.

We settled down to our Christmas together. The following day we went out and did our Christmas shopping. We didn't have a lot of money but I was determined that this would be a great Christmas for us both. In the supermarket Caroline was off getting fruit and sweets for the celebration and I was looking at the turkeys in the freezer. They were so expensive. We had spent nearly all our money on my fares home for weekend leaves. I only got four travel warrants a year and they had been very quickly used. The rest of my trips home at weekends had been at my own expense. I glanced to my right and saw a whole load of turkeys which seemed to be so much cheaper than all the others. I browsed through them. The sign above the freezer said 'Grade B Turkeys'. They were almost half the price of the others. I checked one out. It seemed fine to me and, after all, a supermarket wouldn't be allowed to sell turkeys that were dangerous or anything. I picked out one big enough for the two of us and which would leave plenty over for Boxing Day and sandwiches. Caroline came back with her arms full of goodies.

"I've got the turkey love." I said and we made our way to the checkout.

I only just had enough money to pay for everything in the basket. 'Good job I got that cheap turkey.' I thought to myself.

We walked the two miles home from the shop, wrapped up against the cold, our fingers numb from carrying the heavy bags. We settled down to enjoy Christmas, just the two of us, our first Christmas together alone. The last Christmas, our first as a married couple had been at my brother's place in Aldershot. It had been great fun and we were grateful to them for having us and giving us a break from my aunt's council maisonette, but, when all is said and done, you always want to spend your first Christmas together with just the two of you. So we would make this our best Christmas yet.

The big day dawned and Caroline was up early to put the dinner on, the full works, bird and all the trimmings. Delicious smells emanated from the kitchen for the entire morning and, by lunchtime my mouth was watering so much I thought I was going to have to change my shirt.

"I'm just dishing up love, do you want to come and lay the table for me?" Caroline called from the steamy kitchen.

"Sure thing darling."

I began to put the cutlery and condiments on our cheap dining table, trying to make it look as nice as I could. I put a cracker next to each of our place settings and even lit two candles in the centre of the table.

Caroline came in and looked at me with a smile.

"Do you want a leg or breast? And I mean turkey."

"Oooh, leg for me sweetheart."

"Okay then, I'll have breast then." She said and set off back to the kitchen.

I followed her down the hall.

"Don't you want a leg then?" I asked her.

"Yes, but don't worry, I'll have breast, it really doesn't matter. I don't mind."

"Hang on a minute love, we can both have leg you know, I only want one."

"It's only got one."

"Pardon"

"Look"

She turned the turkey around and she was right, the thing only had one leg.

I must have looked stunned.

"But where's the other one?" I asked, in retrospect a rather stupid question.

By this time Caroline was laughing.

I couldn't believe it. I had bought an amputee turkey. Now I knew why it was so cheap. I'll give the supermarket grade B turkey. We looked at each other and burst out laughing. It was twenty minutes before we had recovered long enough to dish up the dinner and settle down to eat.

The day was wonderful and Boxing Day was spent lazing about the house doing loads of absolutely nothing. That night we went to bed and I fell into a really deep sleep. About five in the morning I was woken by Caroline hitting me in the back.

"Graham, (my real name by the way) it's started."

I rolled over and looked at her, she was clutching her tummy and grimacing.

"My water's have broken, you'd better call the ambulance, and be bloody quick."

Gavin, our first child was born at 12:43 that day. He had timed his arrival to perfection. I was given extended leave and never did go to Glasgow to fight fires. At last, our luck seemed to be changing. After leave and some time with my newly extended family, I returned to Collingwood, finished my qualifying course, and actually managed to pass it. I was now confirmed as a Leading Ordnance Electrical Mechanic.

As soon as the course was over, I returned to Chatham and rejoined Courageous and watched the boat being slowly rebuilt and returned to working order. The work in refit was often boring but I was able to go home most nights. I even bought myself a motorbike to travel to and from work. Things were looking up.

The end of the refit approached and preparations were made for the rededication ceremony. Ratings from the boat were sent to the nearby naval base to train for the onerous guard duty which would be needed. They spent several weeks marching around with their rifles, bayonets fitted, held smartly in the correct position. They even began to look quite smart. It was announced that the mother of the Minister of State for Wales would rededicate the boat. A strange choice in my view as we had only two Welshman on the boat. Parents and family were allowed to attend also.

The day of the ceremony arrived. Nobody had ever seen the Minister's mother and the officer in charge of the guard was, understandably concerned as to whether he would recognise her. It would be a disaster were he to miss her in the crowd and fail to order the guard to give the General Salute. Hurried phone calls were made to Government and it was announced that she would be easily recognisable. An elderly lady who walked with two walking sticks, she would be wearing a lilac two piece suit with matching hat. She walked with a stoop, had white hair and wore glasses. There was a sigh of relief from the assembled officers as a black Ford Granada motor car pulled up at the head of the dock. The crew were fallen in, in three ranks, immaculate in their best suits and highly polished shoes. The guard, complete with white webbing belts and gaiters, gleaming with new blanco and buckles highly polished, waited at the front, rifles at the shoulder and standing to attention. The crowd of families and guests fell into a hushed and respectful silence as an elderly, white haired lady, dressed in a lilac two piece suit and matching hat, wearing glasses and walking with a stoop supported on two sticks made her way slowly down the jetty. She was supported at her left elbow by a tall distinguished gentleman wearing a beautifully pressed blue pinstripe suit. He helped her to negotiate the obstacles which prevail on the side of a naval dry dock. She stopped directly in front of the guard officer and smiled at him. Behind her, Courageous, newly painted and ready for inspection stood proudly, looking every inch the sleek dark messenger of death she was intended to be.

"GUUUAAARD! GENERAL SALUTE, PREEESENT....ARMS!"

The guard brought their rifles to the present in three snappy and well rehearsed movements. The guard officer carried out an immaculate salute with his sword.

"GUUUAAARD! SHOULDEEEERRRR...ARMS!"

The movement was again carried out with immaculate precision. The boys were doing us proud. The guard officer was just about to march forward and present the guard as ready for inspection when the elderly lady leant to one side, smiled and waved.

"Cooee! David! My don't you look smart." And with that she walked past the gobsmacked officer, into the middle of the ranks of the crew and straight up to the leading cook. She pinched his cheek and smiled at him and then turned round to the assembled crowd and proudly announced:

"He's my grandson, he does the cooking for the crew." Assisted by her escort, she proudly made her way to a vacant seat in the front row of the audience. It was the cook's grandmother. Another entry for the Courageous book of misadventures.

Eventually the ceremony was completed, the real VIP having arrived only a few minutes later. The crew was fallen out and allowed to show their proud families around the boat. My parents had never been on a submarine in their life and I was looking forward to showing them where I lived and worked. The tour began and we worked our way around the boat before stopping for a good look around the control room. The periscope was up and I lowered it a little so that my mother could see through it. I moved it around and picked out a ship on the River Medway for her to look at. She handed her handbag to my Dad and pressed her eye to the lens.

"Ooh!" she said, "It's in colour."

Dad and I looked at each other and fell about laughing. Mum couldn't see what was so funny. When I explained to her that all she was looking at was a reflection in a couple of mirrors she excused her remark by explaining:

"Well, all the submarine films I've ever watched have been in black and white."

Well done Mum, cracker.

CHAPTER TWENTY-ONE

The removal van was ready to go. Our few possessions were packed in the back, taking up probably half of the available space. The Navy provided all the furniture for our home, right down to the cutlery and the bed linen. All we had were personal possessions. The van pulled away and left us to our last few hours in Chatham together. Courageous was ready to go back to sea. The dockyard had completed the refit and all the necessary trials had been carried out to the satisfaction of the Navy who were now ready to accept the boat back from the hands of the dockyard. We were to be based at Faslane again and now, all that remained was the task of moving our families north and then taking the boat around the UK coast to its home port.

I had been allocated a married quarter in Helensburgh, about seven miles from the submarine base. Neither Caroline nor I had yet seen our new home and we were due to move in the following day. We were booked on the overnight sleeper from Euston to Glasgow and we should arrive the following morning, hopefully at about the same time as the removal van. We said our goodbyes to the people who had been our neighbours for the last eighteen months and set off. The train journey north was uneventful and we arrived at Glasgow Central Station tired but reasonably happy, until Caroline caught her first glimpse of Glaswegian low life. A wino was standing outside the station, singing to the queue for taxis, in which we were standing. As he sang he deftly urinated over a well dressed city gent in an immaculate suit and demanded money to stop saturating his trousers. Caroline was aghast. Luckily a taxi arrived and I bundled her in, assuring her that this was not the normal behaviour of our Scottish brethren. The journey from Glasgow Queen Street station to Helensburgh was rather quiet and I could see Caroline wondering what the hell Scotland was going to mean for her and Gavin while I was away at sea. After all, her nearest family was now over three hundred miles away. I tried to cheer her up by pointing out the scenery as the train slowly ate up the thirty miles to Helensburgh. The Glasgow outskirts slowly gave way to the River Clyde and as we neared the end of our journey the scenery was spectacular. The river widened into the entrance to lochs and, in the distance were the snow-capped peaks which form the backdrop to the town of Helensburgh itself. The final leg was a short taxi ride to the married quarter. Our arrival did nothing to cheer Caroline up. From our lovely bungalow in the middle of the Kent orchards we found ourselves transported to a concrete lighthouse. Our new home was in the centre of the Churchill married quarters estate. Our house was in the centre of a terrace of about fifteen identical, three storey houses. There was no front garden and the back garden was the size of a very small band aid plaster. The design of the house itself also left a lot to be desired. It was three floors. On the ground floor was a kitchen/diner and a bedroom, on the first floor was the living room and a bedroom and, on the top floor, a bathroom, without windows, and the third bedroom. With a young baby this meant that we would never be able to sleep on the same floor as him. Every time he needed attention in the night we would have to run either up or down stairs. If we were relaxing in the living room and we wanted a coffee or food we would have to go downstairs to the kitchen. The other problem was the toilet and bathroom. On the landing between the ground and first floor was a small toilet, again with no windows. Every time the light was switched on in either the toilet or the top floor bathroom an extractor fan came on, and stayed on for twenty minutes after the light was switched off. It wouldn't have been quite so bad if it had been quiet. For twenty minutes it was like living in the middle of a strafing by twenty stukas. The fan screamed and whistled until finally screeching to a halt only to start again the next time anyone switched the light on. We quickly learned that, if we got up to use either the toilet or bathroom during the night, we did it in the dark. At least that way we could fall back into bed and go straight back to sleep.

Despite the problems with the house we settled in and things were okay, for a while, but the Royal Navy had obviously been taking a close look at my morale level, and it was getting a bit too high for their liking. I was happy and they couldn't have that now, could they?

It had been decided that Courageous would be going to America. We had been selected to trial a new missile system, sub harpoon. We were to spend six months in Charleston and six in San Diego. Although it was a long period away from home I was, to be truthful, looking forward to another trip to The States. I know that sounds selfish but, well, that's why I had joined the Navy, to see the world. Already I had spent more than half of my time under the oceans of the world and seeing next to bugger all.

'LOEM Cooke, Wardroom, LOEM Cooke.'
I made my way through the narrow passageway, past the mess and up the ladder to the control room. I walked past the periscopes and the sonar room and knocked on the wardroom door.
"Come in."
I pushed the curtain aside and walked into the small officer's mess. The Torpedo Officer was sitting at the table and alongside him was the Coxswain.
"Sit down Cooke." Said the Torpedo Officer.
I began to wonder what I had done wrong. There was something about the two of them and the way they were looking down at the table rather than at me that could only mean bad news for someone, and I had a feeling it was going to be me. I settled onto the bench seat on the other

side of the table and looked at them. They looked at me and then at each other. Neither of them wanted to say what they had to say, that much was obvious. I fidgeted in my seat as the silence began to stretch toward the awkward stage. Eventually the Torpedo Officer looked up.

"How's the family?"

"Fine, thank you, sir."

"Settled into the married quarter then?"

Yes thank you, sir."

"And your son, how's he doing?"

"Very well thank you, sir."

"Good to be back after your course?"

"Great thank you, sir."

"Good, good. And how're things in the forends as a leading hand then?"

"Yup, fine thank you, sir."

Jeez, he would soon be asking me about my sex life.

"That's good, very good. Very good indeed."

I glanced at the Coxswain who was sitting there looking down at the table shaking his head.

The Torpedo Officer looked at me and then at the Coxswain.

"Over to you then I think Coxswain."

The poor Coxswain looked at the Torpedo Officer with a look that would have stopped a runaway horse in its tracks.

"Thank you sir. Chas…"

"Yes, Coxswain."

I was getting a bit fed up with this now, I had work to do and I didn't really want to be sitting here playing charades with this pair of idiots. I looked straight into the Coxswains eyes.

"Right then Chas. So everything's okay then is it?"

Bloody hell, he was at it now.

"Fine thank you."

"Good, good."

I looked at the Torpedo Officer.

"Sir, is that it, can I go back to work now or is there anything else you'd like to ask me in relation to my family's welfare, my well being or my job satisfaction?"

"No Cooke, I think that's it for now, thank you for coming."

Puzzled I got up and began to move toward the door. I saw the Coxswain nudge the Torpedo Officer.

"Aah. Cooke, just one more thing. This has just arrived for you. Thought perhaps we ought to give it to you as soon as possible."

He reached out and handed me a slip of paper.

"Thank you sir." I said, and continued out of the door. As the curtain fell back behind me I looked at the paper I had been given. It wasn't just any old bit of paper, it was a bloody draft chit. I stopped in my tracks and read the words without really being able to take them in.

The words 'Dolphin for training' and 'Resolution Port' jumped out of the page at me. Once again drafty was conspiring to ruin my life. According to the chit in my grubby mitt I was leaving Courageous, for good.

I burst back through the curtain. The Coxswain and the Torpedo Officer were still sitting there, waiting for the explosion. I looked at them both, turned on my heel and flounced out with as much dignity as I could muster, after all, one of the three of us had to act in a normal manner over this.

I stormed back to the forends and dropped onto the step just inside the door. Scouse Newell, one of the young trainees that had joined during the refit was working nearby.

"You okay Chas?" he asked.

Yeah, couldn't be better Scouse."

I told him about the draft chit.

"Where are you going then Chas?"

"Back to Dolphin, to train for Polaris, and then to Resolution. They're turning me into a Bomber Queen the bastards."

I read the draft chit again. Apparently there was a shortage of suitably qualified leading hands of my branch and the Polaris submarines were short on crew. As the National Nuclear Deterrent Force they had precedence over every other ship in the Navy when it came to keeping their crew up to full strength. It had been decided that I would be dragged away from my boat, my home and, more importantly, my family so that I could be trained to work in the missile compartment. They had even decided which bomber I was going to.

I dreaded the thought of being a bomber queen. Each boat had two crews, known as port and starboard. One crew took the boat to sea for eight weeks while the other crew did training and took leave. When the boat came back in the two crews worked together for four weeks to prepare it for sea again and then the other crew would take it out for another eight week patrol. This was how the bomber routine went on and on. They never went anywhere except on patrol. They had no visits or runs ashore and it was bloody boring. I had never ever wanted to go on bombers. I had steered away from them like the plague and now, through no fault of my own, I was to be dragged, kicking and screaming, toward a life of tedium. God, I hated the bloody Navy.

The next problem was, how I was going to tell Caroline. Here we were, just settled into life together in Scotland and I was being sent all the way back to Portsmouth for more courses. She was going to be over the moon at this one.

"Chas, does that mean you're going to miss the States trip then?" asked Scouse.

I hadn't even thought of that. Oh god, things just got better and better didn't they.

That evening I went home and, as usual, Caroline took it all in her stride. In her view the training was only about ten weeks and then, when I did eventually join the Resolution, at least we could plan our life a bit. After all, the routine never changed, eight weeks out, twelve weeks home. I couldn't argue with that but, that was the problem, I had never enjoyed predictability. One of the things I really liked about being a submariner was the fact that I rarely knew, from one minute to the next, what I would be doing. Oh, we had a rough idea of the boat's programme, but it was always open to last minute changes. Bombers, well they were so predictable it was untrue. If you wanted to know which of the bombers was going to sea, and when, all you had to do was ask a Helensburgh taxi driver. So much for secrecy surrounding the nation's nuclear deterrent.

It was soon time for me to leave Courageous and head off into the boring world of bomber patrols but, first, there was just one small formality to be concluded, my leaving run. Now a matelot's leaving run is best compared to a stag night, his last night of freedom with the men he has worked alongside for a long period. It is customary to return in a comatose state and to feel the full effects for several days afterwards. Mine was to be no exception. Even Nougat Boomerang, the torpedo officer, came with us. Now that name holds a tale of its own.

Our submarine had a very small office in a dark corner above the oxygen candle store and, because no submarine has a shop onboard, one of the crew was detailed off to run the nutty store or canteen for the boys. On his first trip on Courageous our Torpedo Officer had queued with the crew to buy his sweeties and, on reaching the front of the line was heard to ask for nougat. Now, he pronounced it correctly, 'noogah'. We common seamen however knew it as nougat pronounced 'nuggit'. A discussion took place over the correct pronunciation with everybody, except the Torpedo Officer, insisting it was nuggit. Eventually the keeper of the crew's consumables relented and gave him his 'noogah' but, from that day on the unfortunate officer was known as Noogah. The boomerang bit came later.

Every submarine senior rate's mess has a small bar which serves barrelled beer. Now don't get carried away by the word bar. On a diesel boat it is a tiny cupboard in one corner with a tap in it. On Courageous it was a very small bar with room for one person to stand and serve. On bombers, well, it was a pukkah bar that ran the full width of the senior rates mess with room for an entire host of barmen to serve. The point is that beer reps are always trying to sell huge quantities of beer to these messes and will go to extraordinary lengths to close the sale.

Courageous had received a visit from a rep for Foster's Lager and had placed a small order. To show his boundless gratitude the rep had arranged for an entire selection of Foster's Lager souvenirs to be sent to the crew. These included keyrings, beermats, bartowels, teatowels and a variety of other gifts all in the form of or bearing a picture of a boomerang. In the bottom of the huge box had been found a full sized wooden boomerang, which weighed about three and a half pounds. Needless to say, this had been purloined by the torpedo room crew and adopted as their mascot. Everywhere we went drinking the boomerang had to come with us and tradition dictated that, at some time during the evening's proceedings, the boomerang had to be thrown by a selected member of the party wherever they may be at the time. Generally it was in a bar or restaurant which, if you can imagine a two and a half foot long, three and a half pound lump of good Aussie wood hurtling around a crowded room, tended to cause some considerable upset and normally resulted in a quick getaway by the torpedomen.

Now one night the new Torpedo Officer had been invited to a torpedomen's run ashore. He was nominated to be the bearer of the boomerang and would subsequently become responsible for throwing it at a time and place decided by us. The evening wore on and drink of an alcoholic nature was consumed in great quantities. Torps, as he was known on the boat, poor old Noogah, had done his best to match us drink for drink throughout the evening. We had been getting more and more pissed, he, in the time honoured nature of Naval Officers, had become tired and confused. We began to wend our way back to the base, a four or five mile walk as no taxi driver in his right mind would even consider having us in his vehicle. Suddenly somebody in the group remembered that Noogah was still carrying the boomerang which had not been thrown. A general cry of disapproval erupted and demands were made for the bearer of the boomerang to bung it. Noogah did just that. In his confused state he threw it toward the water of the loch just across the road. Now the problem is that a boomerang comes back and, at the time that he'd thrown it Noogah was standing outside a row of granite houses which had a superb view across the loch toward

Greenock. Unfortunately, inexperienced as he was in the art of boomerang bunging, Noogah had failed to appreciate the kinetic energy in three and a half pounds of curved wood. It sailed majestically out toward the water of the loch before completing a smart about turn and hurtling straight back toward Noogah's face. He did exactly what I suppose every one of us would have done. He ducked. In fact, it would be more accurate to say that, pissed as he was, he tried to get out of the way, tripped over his own feet and fell over, giggling like a three badge parrot. The boomerang flew past his prostrate form with that ominous whistle that fast moving, heavy objects tends to make, and careered through the large front window of the house behind him. We took the only sensible course of action available: we legged it. Not Noogah. Oh no. He took this bearer of the boomerang thing seriously.

"You go on chaps, I'll just retrieve the boomerang and I'll follow on."

Before we could stop him, Noogah was over the low wall, across the garden and clambering through the open space where, not two minutes before, a glazed panel had been in situ. We watched and waited. We could hear Noogah crunching around the room on the shattered remnants of the window now laying in some Scotsman's front room. A light came on in the hallway of the house and we heard shouting. We saw Noogah making a break for freedom through the window frame, only to be dragged back by the irate resident. There was sounds of a scuffle from within and grunts emanated from the house. Eventually Noogah came through the missing window head first, completed a very stylish roll before leaping to his feet and running drunkenly down the path, through the gate and toward us. He had a huge grin on his face which was cut and bruised. One eye was beginning to swell but, give the man his due, he had got the boomerang back. Together we ran for about half a mile before we felt it safe to slow down. A couple of police cars raced up and down the main road as we hid in convenient bushes but, eventually we managed to get back to the base and safety. The next day the MOD police, accompanied by the local constabulary, visited each of the boats in turn to see if anything was known of the burglary the previous night. We kept Noogah hidden in the Forends till they'd given up and from then on his new name stuck. He would forevermore be known as Lieutenant Noogah Boomerang RN.

Anyway, as I previously said, leaving runs are designed to leave the departing crew member comatose and, I have to say, the lads did a pretty good job. I remember nothing of the night out except that the following morning, I awoke curled up in a ball on the front doorstep of my house with Caroline looking over me in her dressing gown. Not only had the milkman left two pints of full cream, someone had delivered me home too. At least they had the good manners to write 'Sorry Caroline' on a bit of paper and push it through the door.

I spent the following two days recovering and then, late Sunday night, set out for Portsmouth and back to the submarine school at HMS Dolphin to learn all about bombers.

Now I have to say, the following two years and three months of my naval career were not the most interesting I'd ever had. No offence to those men who worked in Polaris submarines, they worked as hard as any other submariner, but I hated every minute of it. The boring routine obviously suited some men and, I'm sure, it suited Caroline no end. At least she knew when I was due to be away and when I was going to be home. For the first time since we were married she was able to build a routine into her life. I was bored gutless. Go to sea, come home, go to sea, come home. Never a break in the monotonous routine of life on a bomber. The only way out of it was to go for another promotion and move on. I studied hard and worked toward the promotion I wanted so much.

It was during the long patrols that the much awaited familygram played such a big part in our lives. Bomber crews were privileged, their wives were allowed to write forty words instead of the normal thirty. I'm sure Caroline spent many an evening, sitting at home, struggling over what to say in the latest message to me out at sea. The first two words had to be my name and number so that left Caroline thirty eight words in which to tell me all that happened at home in the last seven days. In addition, no bad news was allowed. If there was any hint of bad news then the familygram was not sent, it was as simple as that. Also, if there was any mention of dates of return or departure it was held back and, if the Navy thought that there was any kind of code in the message, again it would not be sent.

To give the Navy their due, they did try and take care of the crew's welfare. One senior rate received a familygram from home informing him that Fred had died the previous week. It was held back and, on return to Faslane, the Captain was informed that one of the crew had suffered a bereavement. The poor man had realised that there was one weeks familygram missing and had therefore already realised that something was wrong at home. He was called into the Captain's cabin. There the awful news was broken and he was immediately packed off to his home in the South of England with seven days compassionate leave in which to console his grieving family.

On his return, seven days later, he was interviewed by the Captain who was keen to ensure that the man's welfare was thoughtfully considered.

"So Chief, how are you?"

"Yes, I'm fine thank you sir."

"And your family, are they coping alright?"

"Yes sir, they seem to have come to terms with it fairly well, although the kids are still upset."

"And did the funeral go okay, well, as well as these things can go?"

"Yessir, it was really rather nice, just a few words and a burial in the back garden."

"I'm sorry Chief, for a minute there I thought you said the burial was in the back garden."

That's right sir, where else would you bury a golden Labrador?"

"You mean I've just given you a weeks compassionate leave for your bloody dog?"

"I thought you knew sir…."

"Bugger off Chief, and by the way, you owe the navy seven days leave."

The patrol during which that message was received was notable for two other incidents. Firstly I received a familygram to tell me that Caroline was pregnant again and secondly, for the 'Jimmy's a wanker' incident which rather spoilt the atmosphere on the boat.

Every submarine has to have a communication system onboard. On smaller submarines this consists of a loudspeaker system with microphones in all compartments and any other important areas of the boat. In larger, nuclear submarines there is also a telephone system.

Resolution was a big boat. It was over seven thousand tons in weight and had three decks. There were microphones dotted all over the boat and, next to each, was a panel of switches, the operation of which controlled what areas of the submarine received the broadcast message. There was a master switch on each panel which, when selected, made sure that every person onboard could hear the message through any one of hundreds of loudspeakers throughout the boat.

It all began about two weeks into the patrol.

It was early evening and the crew were eating. Those not eating were on watch. The loudspeakers throughout the boat crackled into life and a quiet voice said.

"Do you hear there." The normal lead into an important announcement designed to attract the crew's attention.

Everybody stopped eating, quiet descended on the boat as the whole crew waited for the message.

"The Jimmy is a wanker."

There was a second of dead silence followed by uproar. People were choking on their food laughing.

Again the loudspeakers crackled. Again silence descended on the crew.

"Do you hear there, First Lieutenant speaking. Would the person who called me a wanker report to the control room?"

The reply wasn't long in coming.

"Push off, wanker."

The First Lieutenant burst down the ladder from the control room and into the junior rates dining room. He looked around but nobody was anywhere near the broadcast system.

His search of the boat took some time with no success.

After about an hour there was another broadcast.

"Didn't find me did you, wanker?"

"First Lieutenant speaking, the broadcast system is for emergency and official use only, no more pipes of this nature are to be made."

"It's official then, you are a wanker."

The wanker broadcasts went on and on for the next six weeks. The Captain issued numerous warnings as to the punishment that would be received by the person making the broadcasts, but they continued unabated. The First Lieutenant was clearly agitated by them and he actually lost weight and began to look ill toward the end of the patrol. At various hours throughout the day and night the announcement that "The Jimmy's a wanker." were made for all to hear. The crew were as baffled as the victim. Whoever it was making the broadcasts, for once they were managing to keep the prank to themselves. We even had a book running on the likely culprits.

With only a few days before the end of the patrol and twenty four hours before we were due to surface the First Lieutenant made his way to the wardroom. It is a busy time for the crew as all the preparations have to be made for the secret patrol records to be handed over, the submarine to be cleaned and prepared for maintenance and the handover to the other crew. The Jimmy had a lot on his plate and the 'wanker' broadcasts were doing nothing to help his rising state of anxiety.

He pulled back the curtain of the Captain's cabin, intent on discussing some of the work that needed doing before arrival alongside. He was just in time to find the Captain, hunched over his desk, microphone in his hand making a shipwide broadcast.

"Jimmy's a wanker."

Every single one of us lost our money. I'd laid good odds that it was the Chief Stoker, but the Captain, well, who'd have thought eh?

CHAPTER TWENTY-TWO

We had twelve weeks at home to look forward to. Caroline was pregnant and I was working for promotion. I had refresher training to do and maintenance on the boat until the other crew left for patrol. Then it would be leave for a couple of weeks before back to more training and then, all too soon the boat would be returning and I would be preparing to go away again.

The date of my exam was set for the period while the boat was at sea with the other crew. Again I sat a written exam and another oral examination by a board of the ship's officers. Again, I was successful. Before the boat returned I had become a Petty Officer. My uniform had to be changed, which cost me a fortune, and I was allowed to leave the Junior Rates Mess and join the Senior Rates Mess. I received letters of congratulation from my parents and sisters and I sent them photographs of me, no longer wearing the traditional milk churn lid sailor's hat and collar but, instead, resplendent in peaked white cap and proper brass buttoned jacket. I looked the dog's bollocks, but, when it came down to it, I would have to do the next couple of patrols doing the same job, just earning a little more money for it. I still had a little while to go before I could leave the Resolution and, even then, it wasn't certain that I wouldn't return to bombers. Only drafty knew the answer.

By this time Caroline was ready to burst. She was due to give birth in July and she did just that. Late one night she went into labour and we rushed to the Vale of Leven hospital at the southern end of Loch Lomond. The labour room was quiet, not many people in except us and a couple of other mothers to be. The labour dragged on and then at last, the baby was on its way. It wasn't long before Caroline gave birth to our second son, Paul. The midwife looked at me holding my new son in her arms.

"Congratulations Mr Cooke, it's another boy."

"Thank you. Thank you very much. Brilliant, I'll go and phone the grandparents."

I gave Caroline a kiss and turned to leave the room.

"Where are you going?" said the doctor, "There's another one to come yet."

I was stunned.

"What do you mean another one. We've got it, he's over there." I said pointing to my son, wrapped in a blanket on the scales.

"You may have one already but there's still another one in there waiting to come out." Said the doctor looking at me.

"You mean, twins?"

"Yes Mr Cooke, twins."

"But nobody told us, I've only got one cot and a single pram. Can't you put it back? I can't afford another one." I said which, thinking back on it, was a bloody stupid question.

The doctor just raised his eyebrows and turned back to the job in hand and, within five minutes I had gone from being a father of one to a father of three. We hadn't even thought of a name for the third one.

I left the room to gather my thoughts and get some fresh air. Nobody had even given us any clue that we might be having twins. In fact, Caroline and I had discussed insuring against the expense but, all along we had been told that it was going to be one big healthy baby. I walked out into the hospital grounds to get some fresh air. It was only half past seven in the morning.

"How're ye doin son?"

I looked round and saw one of the expectant fathers. He spoke with a broad Glaswegian accent and was built like a brick shithouse.

"Great thanks." I replied.

"Has ye missus spat it oot yet?" he asked.

"Yeah, she's just had twins. Both boys." I said, still dazed by the enormity of the event.

"Ach, that's bloody greet mon, here have a wee swally a this to help ye alang." And he thrust a bottle of whiskey into my hand.

Now, I don't like whisky, I never have and even the smell of the stuff makes me retch. But, after all, he was six foot four and twice as wide as me. What was I to do. I took a gulp of the hideous contents and held back the bile which rose into my throat.

"Well done son, well done indeed." Said the man and walked off chuckling. I ran round the corner and puked for a full five minutes. I was suffering from shock but I was getting used to the idea already.

I phoned my parents and my brother and sisters to tell them the news before going back into the ward to see Caroline and my two new sons. The doctor was talking to her and she looked worried. I went to stand beside her and could see tears in her eyes.

"Aah, Mr Cooke, I've just been speaking to your wife. There's a slight problem with one of the twins."

My heart sank.

"It's nothing too serious so don't worry about it. The first one out, Paul I believe you've called him, his legs are a little bent and one of his feet is slightly malformed. It was obviously a bit crowded in there," he said patting Caroline's tummy, "and it would seem that the other twin may have been laying on top of him. That has caused the problem with the leg but it's nothing that can't be sorted out with time."

Relief washed over me.

"However," he continued, "he also seems to have a slight problem with his stomach, again nothing to worry about but, we do want to keep him in hospital for a little while. Probably just a couple of weeks or so."

I looked at Caroline who was crying again.

"What's wrong love?" I asked.

The doctor spoke again.

"The problem is Mr Cooke. We can't treat him here. He will have to go to Yorkhill Hospital in Glasgow. Now that means that you will both have to come to a decision. You can go home and look after your other son while your wife goes to Glasgow with the twins. You can take Ian home while your wife goes to Glasgow with Paul or you can both go home with Ian while Paul goes to Glasgow on his own and you can visit him at any time you want to. I'll leave you to decide." And with that he walked out.

Caroline and I discussed the problem at length. Gavin, our eldest was already missing his mum and she was missing him. It was decided, for better or worse, that Caroline and Ian would come home while Paul went to Glasgow alone. We would visit him all day every day until he came home too. It was a difficult decision but we figured that, as a new born baby he would be happy as long as he was warm, fed and cuddled. We could do all of that when we visited and the nurses could look after him while we were away. And so it began. Caroline came home and introduced Gavin to his new brother and we then spent several weeks trekking the thirty miles each way to Glasgow on the train every day.

It wasn't long before Paul came home with us and the only thing we had to worry about was the cast and bar on his legs to straighten his twisted foot. We were a complete family again and Gavin had really taken to his new brothers, helping to feed them and change them when he was with Caroline and even climbing into our bed to watch us feed them at night.

The time for me to return to sea was drawing closer and closer. It would be harder for all of us this time. We had drawn the short straw and I would be away over both Christmas and the New Year, a time when any family wants to be together. The time flew by as the preparations for the patrol carried on apace. The boat was hauled round to Coulport, where we loaded the necessary missiles for the trip. Soon the day to leave came around and I said goodbye to Caroline and the boys on the doorstep before climbing onto the coach for the trip round to the boat. This was going to be a bastard of a trip and the atmosphere on the coach, and on the boat, was one of general gloom. Nobody likes to leave their family for eight weeks and especially so over the festive season.

'This is going to be a long eight weeks.' I thought to myself as I clambered down the hatch and took my last glimpse of daylight for two months or so. It was freezing cold and the hills were covered in a fine dusting of snow. Inside the boat it was, as normal, muggy and warm, bright fluorescent light and nothing natural about anything. I seriously considered giving it all up and trying to live a normal life with Caroline and the kids.

The patrol dragged on and eventually Christmas day arrived. To be fair, everyone was trying hard to get into the festive spirit and as we all sat down for dinner, those who weren't on watch anyway, Naval tradition dropped into place and the officers appeared and began to serve the junior rate's meal, the youngest crew member traditionally served by the Captain. The plates were piled high with festive fare and everyone was ready to tuck in, even crackers had been supplied to add to the festive cheer. Suddenly the raucous buzz of the general alarm stabbed through the cacophony of jeers and cheers. There was instant silence.

"Action stations, action stations. Action stations missile. Set condition 1SQ."

It was absolutely unbelievable. Throughout the eight week patrol an unknown number of test firing signals would be sent by the MOD at Northwood and the submarine would go through the drill for firing a series of missiles. No matter where we were, what we were doing or what time of day it was, the entire crew had to turn to and close up as though for real. Some arse in the MOD had obviously decided that lunchtime on Christmas day would be the ideal time to send the crew of Resolution to action stations. Whoever that idiot was he did more to lower crew morale than an entire series of disasters onboard could have done. If it had been a flood or fire then we could have understood the need to miss our rapidly congealing meal but to practise something we could do with our eyes shut at the whim of some dick-head took the biscuit. Christmas day was ruined and even the Captain was looking pretty annoyed by it all.

The rest of the day was a waste of time. It was over an hour before the crew were able to sit down and eat their meal which, by then, had cooled beyond edibility. I hope that whoever prompted the exercise had a damned miserable life. He ruined the only day of celebration for one hundred and forty men on that boat.

With Christmas over the only highlight of the patrol to look forward to was New Year. It never ceased to amaze me that men could get a set of bagpipes into a submarine and actually practise without being killed by the crew. But manage they did and the New Year was seen in by the traditional Scottish Hogmanay piper and first footing all around the boat. Many a beer was drunk that night and there were a few sore heads on the first day of 1981.

Caroline's familygrams were arriving on pretty much the same day of each week and I looked forward to them with disproportionate pleasure. It is amazing how much forty typed words can mean to a man who is totally shut off from the real world for two months.

To be fair to Caroline, life was much harder for her at home than it was for me. After all, I didn't get bills in the post and have to worry about what to buy for the next week's meals. It was surprising that nearly all familygrams began with the same words, no matter who sent it. They went something along the lines of:
'POWEM   COOKE-D136038Y-DARLING-GRAHAM-WEATHER-LOVELY...
Weather lovely? Who the hell wanted to know that? I wasn't even allowed to look through the periscope on a bomber so I couldn't even see fresh air, let alone smell it. The last thing I wanted to know was how

nice the weather was. But this patrol Caroline's familygrams were more downbeat and I began to sense that something wasn't quite right at home. It is amazing how much you can glean from thirty eight typed words on a strip of paper without the author actually saying anything is wrong. I became more and more convinced as the patrol went on that something was not quite right but what could I do out here? A bomber will never come in from its patrol area, even if one of the crew dies. It was told, and I have it from good authority that it was true, that one wife, accompanied by her children, came to see her husband off to sea and, on the way home the wife and children were killed in a car accident. The husband was only told on the day that the boat arrived back after the eight week patrol, by which time his wife and children were buried. That shows you just how much importance the Navy and the Government place on the maintenance of a continuous deterrent patrol by the bombers.

After what seemed an age Resolution surfaced and made her way back to Coulport where she would unload her missiles before moving back round to Faslane. It was always arranged that the other crew took over the watches for the first night, even though we still officially had command of the boat. That meant that everyone who had been on patrol could go home on the first night in. I waited impatiently for the bus to set off back toward Helensburgh and the journey seemed to take forever. We weren't allowed to drive for at least twenty four hours because of the loss of distance perception. We spent eight weeks in artificial light and even medium level daylight seemed to dazzle us. For two months we had been able to see only short distances so to see for miles across the lochs and hills of the highlands was strange in the extreme.

At long last the coach pulled into the square outside my house and there was Caroline, standing on the doorstep, a huge grin on her face. I ran the last few yards and hugged her and Gavin who was in her arms. The twins were asleep and I would see them later. I looked at Caroline. She looked tired, in fact she looked exhausted. Slowly the story came out. She had been told to take Paul to hospital every Friday morning and she did just that. She pushed a twin pram and pulled a buggy, containing Gavin, two miles to Helensburgh station. She then fought her way onto the train with them. At Glasgow Queen Street she had to struggle off the train with them and then get them up two flights of steps to ground level. Then she had a two mile walk to the hospital, again pushing the pram and pulling the buggy. After Paul had received his treatment, the whole journey had to be completed in reverse. It took nearly six hours to do it all and the strain was showing. The Navy had done nothing to help, despite knowing of the problems, and I hit the roof.

Worse was to come. During the patrol I had missed a whole host of family events, the birthdays of my brother, my wife, my son and myself. We stood in the kitchen. Caroline looked up at me and said.

"Happy birthday, Merry Christmas, Happy New Year and by the way, your grandmother's dead."

My great grandmother, of whom I thought the world, had died two weeks into the patrol. She was ninety nine years old and had been looking forward to her telegram from the queen. I had missed her funeral and had not had a chance to say my goodbyes. Such is the life of a submariner.

The following day I went into work and requested that I be allowed to miss the next patrol to give Caroline a rest. My request was refused. I complained and my complaint was thrown out. Eventually I kicked up such a stink that the welfare people became involved and, early one morning, Caroline and I received a visit from a hard faced woman who said she was the one who made the decisions. We explained the circumstances and she sneered at me and said,

"I see no reason to allow you to stay home for the next patrol period. I'm sure if she puts her mind to it your wife will cope very well."

I nearly hit the woman. Who the hell did she think she was.

"I don't accept that." I said, "You haven't got the faintest idea what this is doing to us as a family have you?"

I looked at her left hand and saw no rings.

"Are you married?" I asked.

She looked sheepish and replied in the negative.

"Have you even had any experience of dealing with children yourself?" I pressed.

Again she shook her head.

"So how the hell can you tell my wife that 'she'll cope'?" I demanded.

"Petty Officer Cooke, if you feel that you really have to stay at home while your submarine goes to sea on the next patrol, then I will recommend a discharge from the service on welfare grounds." She said looking at her notepad.

This was it. I had considered it anyway so what the hell?

"Where do I sign then?" I asked.

She looked stunned.

"Come on then, you made me an offer and I'm accepting, where do I sign to get out?"

She began to back pedal then and, all of a sudden she was offering to speak to my Commanding Officer and see what she could do.

The following morning I was called into the Captain's cabin and handed a draft chit. I had to do my Petty Officer's Qualifying Course in Portsmouth at some time so they had brought it forward by a few months. I was to take my family to Portsmouth. After I had spent the next patrol at home taking care of them and sorting out the move. I'd called her bluff and I'd won. It was the first time for ages that I had been able to give Caroline any genuinely good news.

It was at this point that life began to take a turn for the better. Firstly Caroline and I managed to rent a house owned by a housing society who rented solely to naval personnel. The good thing was that it was in Bridgemary, away from the married quarters at Rowner Estate which was known, throughout the Navy, as The Concrete Jungle. Once more we moved into a house we had never seen before we opened the door to insert our furniture. This time we had complete freedom to decorate the house as we wanted to. We were no longer tied by the strict rules rigidly enforced in married quarters where only pastel paint was allowed on the walls and every hole you made to hang a picture cost you ten pence when you moved out. The house was only thirty minutes walk or ten minutes cycle ride from Collingwood where, once again I was under training. At least on this course I was a Petty Officer, a senior naval rating and treated very much like an adult. We had our own mess complete with bar and social facilities. The food was the same at meals but the décor was so much better. No compulsory sport on Wednesday afternoon. We were allowed off the base to play golf or go swimming once a week and life was just so much more civilised. We even had regular mess dinners with a guest speaker and silver service.

The best thing about the mess dinners were the letters of apology on the mess notice board the following morning. One in particular I found amusing. The guest speaker had been the well known entertainer, Tommy Trinder, famous for the trilby hat which he wore on all occasions. To give the after dinner speech, Mr Trinder had removed his hat and placed the precious article, carefully out of harms way, on the floor beside his chair. The letter displayed the next morning went like this:

'To The president & Members of The Petty Officer's Mess, HMS Collingwood.

Sir,

I would like to thank you for a superb evening last night when I enjoyed tremendously the very successful mess dinner. I would, however, like to apologise for my disgraceful behaviour and any consternation I may have caused to you or our honoured guest, by inadvertently vomiting into Mr Trinder's trilby hat during his speech. I will, of course, be prepared to pay for either specialist cleansing of said trilby or a replacement item.

I am sir,

Your obedient servant
****
Petty Officer.'

I was now only duty once in a blue moon and that meant that I had almost every evening and all weekend at home with the family. Paul's regular visit to the Naval Hospital Haslar, a short bus ride away, were proving beneficial. On our first visit there the naval doctor had taken one look at the metal splints and bars holding Paul's feet in shape and told us to get that 'scrap iron off his legs, get him walking and as soon as he can, kicking a ball and he'll be fine.'

We settled down into domestic routine of being a family together but I still had the Sword of Damocles hanging over me. What was in store for me at the end of the course? For all we knew I could be sent back to the bombers in Faslane, fleet boats at the same base, fleet boats in Plymouth or diesel boats in any one of four places, Rosyth near Edinburgh, Faslane or Plymouth or here in Portsmouth. The First Submarine Squadron which consisted of the greatest number of diesel boats was based right here at HMS Dolphin, it was more than I could realistically hope for. I had spent my entire submarine career in nuclear submarines and surely the Navy wouldn't want to waste all the money they had spent on training me for that role.

As the course came toward a close, other's in my class began to receive their draft chits with a mixture of relief or disgust, dependant upon whether their wishes and drafty's were the same. I was the only submariner in my class of eighteen Petty Officers and everyone else knew where they were going. A sense of foreboding fell over me as time dragged by. Eventually I was called in to see my Divisional Officer.

"Come in Petty Officer Cooke, I've got your draft chit here." He said passing across the by now familiar piece of paper. I didn't know whether to open it now or later.

"Once you've read it I have a supplementary notice here from Drafty and I'll explain what's going on Cooke."

I looked at the chit in my hand and opened it. I was shaking like a leaf. So much for me being a big roughy toughy sailor.

It read:

'Petty Officer Weapons Engineering Mechanic (Ordnance) (Submarines) Cooke D136038Y. To join HMS Coillingwood for Instructor and Divisional senior Rate duties immediately upon satisfactory completion of Petty Officer's Qualifying Course.'

Well. That was the last thing I was expecting. Did this mean that I was no longer a submariner. Had I been kicked out of the submarine service? What the hell was going on?

"Take a seat Chas and I'll explain the supplementary part of all this." Said my Divisional Officer offering me a chair.

"You look a bit baffled by this Chas."

"I am sir. I wasn't expecting to stay here. That was the last thing that crossed my mind to be honest."

He smiled and explained.

"What are you like with torpedo's Chas? I hear you're pretty experienced in that field."

"I suppose I am sir, I've spent most of my time in the Navy as a torpedoman or working with weapons of some kind."

"Well the Navy obviously think so too. As you may be aware, the Navy's Underwater Weapons Branch is being phased out. As you are no doubt aware, they have always been responsible for all sub surface weapons, both in the surface fleet and, as Torpedo Instructors, in the Submarine Service. With them going the Navy has had to find someone to take their place and it has only just been announced that the WEM(O) branch will be taking over their responsibilities. What that means for you is that yourself, and a Petty Officer Makin, are to be the first two electrical ratings to be trained as Torpedo Instructors. You begin a two man course at HMS Dolphin in three months time, on completion of which you will both join the First Sub Squadron at Dolphin as TIs. In the interim we have asked that you remain here and train some of our new recruits in basic electrical skills. How does that suit you?"

How did that suit me? I could not have been happier. I wasn't going back to bombers. I wasn't even going back to Faslane or Scotland. I was going to be based here in Portsmouth with my family settled and happy and, what was more, I had joined the Navy on the same day as Phil Makin and we were good mates who had followed each other around the service. I was probably, at that moment, the happiest little Petty Officer in ten men's navies.

"That's really good sir. Thank you. It's pretty much what I'd hoped for."

I had suddenly become the king of understatement.

"Good, see you at the end of the course and good luck Chas."

"Thank you, sir. Thank you very much." I replied and walked out into the bright sunshine of a brilliant day.

The first thing I did was run to the mess and phone Caroline. She was as happy as I was with the news. Next I phoned Phil and we had a chat about the future course. We both agreed to get together for a drink before the course began and renew our friendship.

Two weeks later I completed the Qualifying Course and was confirmed in the rank of Petty officer. My branch badge now had a golden crown above it. It didn't mean much really other than a very small pay rise and, if I managed to get in the shit sometime in the future it was harder for the navy to bust me down a rank or two.

Even the three months training young sprogs was a bit of a laugh. I actually got hauled up in front of the training commander because I spent every afternoon out on the sports field with my class playing football or softball. Somebody, probably one of the other instructors, and no doubt a skimmer too, had complained. His class were studying hard toward their exams each week while mine were outside in the sun enjoying themselves. I pointed out to the commander that all he had to do was look at the exam results and, if my class were worse than average I would stop all sport and relaxation. He duly checked the figures and found that my lads were actually top in every exam since I took over. I was given official clearance to carry on with the sports. In my view, and by the time I finished talking to the commander he agreed, the attention span of the average recruit was about thirty minutes at most and they had an awful lot to take in. I had regular breaks but by lunch time they were sick to death of sitting in a stuffy classroom listening to my voice so, if I gave them an hour or so outside and something to increase their heart rate and adrenalin level, they would spend the last hour swotting like Trojans. It certainly seemed to work because twenty one of my class of twenty two were in the top thirty for the whole course. These skimmers had a lot to learn about relaxing and enjoying life. When it came to having a good laugh some of the instructors were so slow they nearly met themselves coming back.

My course came to an end and I sent my green little sprogs off to join the fleet. God help them, and the fleet. Now it was my turn. I wended my way off to HMS Dolphin, there to start my new life as a Torpedo Instructor. With only two of us on the course it was so laid back we were almost horizontal. The only problem was that it takes more than two people to sling a ton and a half of torpedo around the front end of a submarine. Luckily there was a basic torpedoman's course running at the same time so Phil and I took it in turns to take charge of them. At times it was akin to Fred Karno's Circus but we were getting there and having damned good fun doing it. We were sent off to learn how to blow things up, we were taught how to account for every single bullet and bomb held or used on the boat and a host of other subjects we had to master before being allowed to take charge of a torpedo compartment. For practical experience we used HMS Grampus, an old diesel submarine that had been taken out of active service and was now used as a training boat, alongside at Dolphin. Diesel boats were at best agricultural and, in some respects, bloody dangerous, but Phil and I were both looking forward to getting on one and doing the job for real. The time was almost upon us and we both received our drafts on the same day. Phil was sent to Onyx and I was given Onslaught, both attached to the First Sub Squadron at Dolphin. Once again I was able to give Caroline good news. We were staying where we were and Gavin, who had just started school, would not have to be uprooted and start all over again somewhere else. The navy really seemed to be doing things to suit me for a change.

CHAPTER TWENTY-THREE

Now I feel that I need to explain a few things about diesel boats. They were definitely not built with the comfort of the crew in mind. If it were a recipe it would read something like this. Take three carriages of an underground train. Weld together and remove all windows. Now add miles of pipework containing air, seawater, freshwater and hydraulic oil, all at high pressure and stir in a generous amount of electrical wiring. Add round doors approximately four feet across at regular intervals. Add sparingly a small number of toilets, four should be plenty, and two bathrooms. Ensure that bathrooms are not used whilst at sea. On the bottom of the mixture place 448 batteries, approximately 224 tons in weight and, toward the back of the mixture carefully place two very large sixteen cylinder mechanically supercharged diesel engines. At the front and rear of the mixture place enough tubes to fire torpedoes, eight is ample, six at the front and two at the back. Liberally scatter large boxes of electrical and mechanical equipment throughout the entire mixture and finally, as a garnish, add 83 large men with enough equipment for ten weeks away from home. As a final touch insert into the final mixture approximately twenty two torpedoes each carrying half a ton of explosives and stir well. Leave to settle and then place the entire mixture hundreds of feet under water. Leave the mixture to fester for several weeks in the cold and dark.

I hope you get the idea. Diesel boats are fairly basic and take many people by surprise the first time they see them. Approximately three hundred feet long and thirty feet wide it is akin to going to sea on a pencil. They pitch roll and yaw heavily in the slightest sea when on the surface and, if you suffer from sea sickness, should be avoided at all costs. With only one deck on which the whole crew must eat, sleep, socialise and work, conditions are fairly cramped. The senior rates mess on Onslaught was about 12 feet by 9 and was home to twenty eight men, for anything up to six months on an extended trip. The bunks doubled as seats and the passageways in the boat were also filled with bunks. My sleeping berth on the boat consisted of a bunk in the passageway. It was the top one of three with the curve of the pressure hull cutting down the headroom to about nine inches. It was too short and too narrow for me to stretch out on and I could only sleep half on my back, half on my side with my knees and elbows protruding into the passage. Every time somebody walked past in the dark I would be woken by them bumping into me. In addition, directly opposite was the senior rates mess so there was, unavoidably, a fair amount of noise from that. Toward the bottom of the bed was the galley where cooking was taking place most of the day and night with the resultant clattering and banging and, opposite my head was the accommodation space hatch where any rubbish not able to be ejected over board was kept and, after several weeks began to smell. Nuclear submariners have showers and a laundry. There are no such comforts for a diesel boat submariner. He does not wash from the day the boat sails until the day it gets alongside again. He sleeps in his clothes and only ever takes off his boots. There is nowhere to wash clothes so the same ones are worn for the entire trip. Basically, we stank to high heaven. We didn't notice of course, we all smelt the same.

Add to the rank atmosphere the problems of breathing. A nuclear boat makes oxygen from the seawater around it. Diesel boats do not have the room for the equipment to do that so, the only way to change the air is to surface and open the hatches, which rather gives the game away, or to come to periscope depth and run the diesel engines, sucking air in from outside through a tube. The Germans invented this system, known then as a schnorkel, now called a snort induction mast. The exhaust gases are also sent back to the open air above the water, by means of a snort exhaust mast at the top of the boat, so as not to kill the crew by poisoning them with carbon monoxide. This is also how a submarine's batteries are charged, using generators attached to the rear of the engines. It is a physically demanding and dangerous task and it is done, as a rule, every night on a diesel submarine, in which the batteries are the crew's lifeline. No battery charge equals no power, equals no propulsion, equals no live crew. The one advantage to all of this is that, whilst using the batteries to turn electric motors to drive the propellers, a diesel submarine is so quiet as to be just about undetectable. Using her passive sonar, Onslaught could go anywhere without being detected; we could hear and not be heard. The only thing that could give us away was any noise made by the crew itself. Water carries sound much better than air and any noise can be heard for miles. When Onslaught was in the 'Ultra Quiet State' even fluorescent lights were switched off to stop the slight hum that they give off. Men not required for work lay on their beds or sat in their allotted position reading. All orders and replies were whispered and any noise was met with glares from the men.

As the boat remains deep the air slowly becomes more and more foul. Oxygen was produced by burning large candle like cyclinders under extreme pressure and the contents were designed to produce breathable oxygen for the crew. Carbon dioxide was removed by drawing the air through canisters containing soda lime in an attempt to stay deep for longer but, eventually, sometimes after two or three days, the boat would have to return to periscope depth and risk running the diesel engines to charge those vital batteries and renew the air in the boat.

Diesel submariners work a two shift system, six hours on, six hours off, seven days a week for as long as the boat is dived. My six hours on watch were spent in the control room, three hours of steering and depth keeping followed by three hours of contact evaluation. In my six hours off I also had my own department, the torpedo compartment, to look after, and I had to eat and drink so I actually slept for three hours at a time, twice a day. Add to that any time at action stations or emergency stations, all of which mean the entire crew has to be up and working, and you can imagine the conditions on a diesel boat. Most of the crew worked an average of over one hundred hours a week for anything up to eight weeks at a stretch. And people wonder why diesel boat crews tend to let rip a bit when they are ashore.

It wasn't long before I saw the crew of Onslaught in action. We were on our way to Emden in Germany for a 'courtesy visit'. As normal we had been allocated hotel accommodation in the town while we were alongside.

Bernie was a stoker, he was not blessed with the greatest of brains but he was a nice bloke and everyone in the crew got on with him. The problem with Bernie was, he was always broke and looking for ways to make money. Germany is a little more relaxed than the UK when it comes to sex and the sale of sex paraphernalia and Bernie decided that, bearing in mind the normal male frustrations experienced by the crew at sea, he could make an absolute killing if he bought an inflatable sex doll and rented it out to the crew. Now I know what you are thinking and, to be honest, I believe the majority of the crew would agree with you. After all, when all's said and done, even submariners are human and will draw the line somewhere. But Bernie could not be told. He even made up a sign, in his best handwriting, using bright coloured felt tip pens. "Fifty pence a go, first one to spot its nose running empties it.' Not, I have to say, a sign which would instill a sense of sexual desire in most men. Bernie was not a selfish man but, I suppose justifiably, he felt that it would be fair if he were to have one night with the woman of his dreams before he sold her into prostitution amongst the crew. We had been out consuming huge quantities of beer and had collapsed into bed to sleep it off. We had not been in bed long when we were awoken by a strange rhythmic squealing noise. Doors opened all along the hotel passages and a selection of guests, ranging from drunken submariners to fatigued businessmen, were wandering toward the stairway in search of the noise. I had almost reached the stairs when I heard a guttural stream of German coming from below. I couldn't speak any of the language but just the tone of it was enough to make me realise that the words were uttered by somebody who was rather unhappy with something. I looked over the balcony and there, halfway up the grand staircase, stark naked, was Bernie. His backside was pumping up and down and beneath him was the wide armed, open mouthed inflatable doll, bouncing away in latex lust. The stairs were tiled and with every thrust of Bernie's not inconsiderable backside, the latex doll emitted a screech as she was rubbed across the vinyl surface.

"Otto. Kom." I heard and a large Alsatian dog appeared beside the hotel owner. With a flick of his wrist the owner set the dog on the pair of fornicating figures on the stairs. Unfortunately the dog decided to attack the one that was making the most noise first, the doll. Its fangs sank into the hip of the bouncing babe and, with a hideous farting sound, she withered and deflated beneath the humping Bernie. The dog, surprised by the noise and the gush of air, ran whimpering back into the owner's accommodation leaving Bernie frustrated and unfulfilled.

"You bastard," he screamed, clambering to his feet, genitals in full view of the, by this time, considerable audience, "You've burst my woman." And with that he made a lunge for the owner's throat. Luckily he was intercepted by two of his stoker colleagues who dragged him, kicking and screaming, back to his room. He was a sorry sight, pulled backwards down the passageway, his lilywhite naked body glowing in the stark electric light and the love of his life, now fully deflated, dragged along the floor behind him, her hand in his. Several of us managed to placate the irate owner and assured him that we would keep Bernie under control. I made my way to his room to make sure that he would not be repeating the performance and entered only to find Bernie, with a puncture repair outfit, complete with French chalk and rubber patches, desperately trying to plug the gaps in his now shredded sweetheart's lower anatomy. Another of Bernie's fortune making ventures had been brought to an untimely end.

It was not to be the end of Bernie's adventures in Emden. The day we sailed I was checking the equipment in the after torpedo room when I heard a huge roar from the stoker's mess just around the corner by the after escape tower. Curious, I knocked and went in. Bernie was standing on the table, once again he was naked from the waist down. He had his back to me.

"Bernie, what is it with you and getting your tackle out?" I asked.

People were pointing and grimacing toward his genitals. Bernie turned round and I unconsciously crossed my legs and winced. There, through his foreskin, was what I believe is called an Albert ring. He had had his foreskin pierced and a large gold ring put through it.

"Bernie, you are definitely off your trolley." I said, and turned to walk out.

It wasn't long before the whole crew became aware of Bernie's appendage. It went round like a bush fire, everybody wanted to see it but nobody really wanted to ask. It wasn't long before events took a turn for the worse.

I was on watch in the control room and we were on the surface and heading back to the UK. Bernie had been in the after corner for half an hour or more. He wasn't on watch but he was talking to the stoker who was working the hydraulic sytems and masts from the panel in that corner. The conversation was getting more and more heated. I was unable to hear what was being said but Bernie was obviously getting annoyed. It was slowly becoming more and more likely that a fight would break out, and they were only a few feet from the Captain's cabin. I felt it prudent to intervene and calm things down and, stepping between them, I pulled the two apart.

"Bernie," I asked, "What are you doing here? You're off watch and you're making enough noise to wake the dead. Get back to your mess and, whatever your gripe is, talk about it later."

"But it bloody hurts TI, he won't tell me where it is."

Bernie, what hurts and he won't tell you where what is?"

My knob hurts and he won't tell me where the key is."

I was struggling here. I hadn't got a clue what he was on about.

"Bernie, hang on, just tell me what is wrong, preferably in a way that I'll be able to understand. What the hell are you walloping on about." I said, trying to calm him down.

"I'll show you what I'm on about TI." And, with a flourish Bernie dropped his trousers. My eyes must have popped out of my head.

"Now do you see what I mean?" He demanded.

There, where the gold ring had previously been, was a very large, very strong, Chubb security padlock. It must have weighed about a pound and it was stretching his foreskin almost to his knees.

"The lads in the mess held me down, took my ring out and put this in its place TI. Now they won't give me the key to unlock it."

Unfortunately it was at that moment that the Captain decided to come out of his cabin and see what all the commotion was about. He took one look at Bernie's elongated penis, looked at me and said, "TI, I don't know what this is about, I don't want to know what this is about, but you and the Chief Stoker will make sure that it is sorted, understood?"

"Yes sir." I replied to his back as returned to his cabin, shaking his head.

"Bernie, you are a wanker." I stated, now angry at being bollocked by the Captain.

"That's just it TI. I am not a wanker and I will never be a wanker again unless this bastard gives me the key to this padlock."

"Robby, give him the key."

"No TI."

"Robby, I am not messing about; if you do not give him the key I will stick you on for disobeying a direct order. Now, I am ordering you to give him the key."

"I can't TI."

"What do you mean you can't? If it's in your locker, go and get it. If someone else has it, get them to give Bernie the key."

"No TI, you don't understand. I can't give him the key because I threw it over the side."

"You did what?"

This was unbelievable. Bernie looked as though he was going to cry. He began to protest.

"What am I going to say to my wife when I get home with this on me dick? Sorry darling I can't make love to you until the fire brigade have cut this padlock off me knob."

I tried to calm him down.

"Bernie, go back to your mess, I'll get hold of the Chief stoker and we'll see if we can sort this out, and you," I turned to Robby but couldn't carry on, I couldn't hold back the laughter any more and just walked away, tears streaming down my face.

The Chief Stoker was called and he and I retired to the bathroom with Bernie where we inspected the padlock. The bright yellow rubber gloves we wore to inspect the offending article made us look like a couple of demented doctors as we turned it round and inspected it from all angles. It was no ordinary padlock. It was tempered steel and of the type used on the gun lockers. This would not be easy. The Chief Tiff was called to assist in the inspection. Even the Engineer Officer took his turn. It was amazing how many men decided that they needed to wash their hands during the time we were in the bathroom, even though they had been at sea for weeks and knew that there was no water. Everyone wanted to have a look at Bernie's attachment.

By this time things were getting serious. Bernie's penis was turning a funny mottled blue colour and it was obvious that something had to be done, and quick.

"Bernie," said the Chief Stoker, "It's going to have to be hack sawed off, that's the only way."

Bernie looked almost relieved.

"Well alright, but can you do it quickly please, it really hurts now." Pleaded the unfortunate stoker.

"I ain't doing it Bernie. If I slip I could take your knob off mate. No. You'll have to do it yourself."

Bernie retreated to the only vice on the boat. It was in the engine room. The vice was slightly above waist height and was between the back ends of the engines. Bernie was standing on tiptoe, naked from the waist down with the vice in the padlock and his foreskin stretched beyond all recognition. The sea was quite rough and, as the boat rolled Bernie rolled with it. Unfortunately his penis, held firmly in place by the padlock, clamped in the vice, did not roll with him. Every time the boat rolled to port Bernie moved farther from the vice and emitted a pained squeal. He was hack sawing for all he was worth but, as we all know, when you hack saw metal it gets very hot. By the time he had managed to release himself almost an hour later, Bernie was burnt and blistered in places no man wants to be burnt and blistered. The next stop was the Coxswain who issued Bernie with some salve to cool the burns and reduce the blistering.

Bernie never did put his Albert ring back in place. I wonder what his wife said when he got home with a swollen penis with an extra hole in the end.

CHAPTER TWENTY-FOUR

We were soon restored, replenished and redeployed. Diesel boats tend, on the whole, to do shorter trips than their nuclear counterparts and also spend less time alongside before setting to sea again. I had by now settled into the routine of life on a diesel boat. Dirty, damp and dank they may have been but there was a real feeling of camaraderie amongst the crew. There was always something going on at sea and there was always someone in the middle of a wind up somewhere on the boat. I was not averse to a bit of fun myself and Mick Harrow, the Ordnance Artificer, and I were always good for a bit of fun, although those on the receiving end of our latest venture may not have thought it quite so funny.

Mick and I, for several weeks now, had been operating the Bazooka. What, I hear you ask, is a submarine doing armed with a Bazooka. I shall explain. The item in question was a six foot length of black rubber, about a quarter of an inch wide at the centre and tapering to a point at one end. We used it to catch the unwary by surprise in the dimly lit confines of the boat. Mick would stand in front of me with one end of the rubber band in his hand and stretched as far forward as possible. I would be behind him, pulling the other end back to its full extent.

Mick would aim at our unfortunate victim and, on his command of 'Fire' I would release my end of the rubber. It was like flicking a huge elastic band at someone but this one had been known to lay flesh open. The shouts of pain and the resultant uproar had disturbed many a sleeping submariner.

Onslaught had one man onboard, and to save his embarrassment I will not reveal his name in any form, who was not the least bashful when it came to relieving the sexual frustrations of being away from his wife. Not for him the civilised wankerchief and a bit of privacy behind the curtain of his bunk. Oh no, this man would masturbate wherever he felt the urge. At first it was disconcerting to realise what he was up to when you were forced to sit next to him on watch but, as with all things in submarines, the unusual becomes the norm. Mick and I were on watch together and, having finished our last ciggie and a brew from the mess we made our way to the control room to take over from the others. It was one o'clock in the morning, normal watch changeover time, and it was dark outside on the surface. The boat was at periscope depth with both diesel engines running at full tilt to charge the batteries. At the same time any other noisy evolutions were also carried out, blowing the sewage tank overboard, pumping bilges, ditching gash and carrying out any noisy repairs which needed to be done. The control room was in black lighting, not a single light on anywhere. Double layered blackout curtains were rigged at either entrance to the control room to prevent even the smallest amount of light from entering. It was vital that the periscope was manned at all times while at periscope depth and the smallest chink of light could ruin the periscope officer's night vision. Mick and I stood at the forward end of the control room to try and adjust our senses to the pitch dark before trying to move in and take over the watch. The control room itself was fairly quiet with just the muffled sound of the diesels throbbing away, just aft in the engine room. Over the background noise I began to sense another sound. Mick had heard it as well. From the one man control, where a senior rate maintained depth and course, came the unmistakable sounds of masturbation.

Mick turned to me and whispered in my ear.

"The dirty sod's at it again. Go and get the Bazooka, quick."

I made my way, as fast as I could, back to the torpedo compartment and collected the lethal length of rubber from its hiding place. Making my way back into the control room I bumped into Mick's back and handed him his end of the weapon. I pulled back as hard as I could and Mick aimed his end in the general direction of the offensive noises coming from the one man control.

"Fire" he whispered.

I let go of my end and there was a gunshot like crack as the business end of the Bazooka struck the intended victim. There was a muffled grunt and the boat began to point toward the sea bed. The snort induction mast dipped under the water and there was the sound of water rushing down the mast and the unmistakeable sound of the emergency flap valve, designed to stop the boat flooding, slamming shut. The engines began to suck air from the only place left available to them, the boat itself.

"Stop snorting stop snorting stop snorting."

The crew in the control room and engine room crash stopped the engines and shut down the snort system. The boat was still heading down into the depths and the angle of dive was increasing. A few lights came on as the periscope went down and the Captain came running into the control room. In the dim light we could see the guilty senior rate collapsed over the yoke of the depth keeping controls. The yoke was fully forward and people were desperately trying to pull him off and regain control of the boat. He was clutching his testicles which, even in the little light available, were obviously swelling before our eyes. I turned to Mick who, by this time had stuffed the Bazooka into his pocket out of sight. He was looking a bit sheepish and a little pale. I have no doubt that I looked the same, we could have killed us all.

Eventually the injured man was hauled out of the cramped seat and control of the boat was regained. We had reached almost seven hundred feet by the time it was all sorted out. The enquiry never did find out what had caused the sudden collapse of the unfortunate man but, needles to say, the Bazooka was never again to see the light of day.

A week or so later and we were in the Mediterranean. We called into Gibraltar for a short stay but this time I was hardly able to step ashore. We were scheduled to do some training with the Special Boat Service, the Royal Marine's waterborne version of the SAS. Now these men are seriously mad. To even consider doing some of the things they do would be enough to cause most people to call for a psychiatrist. They were fit, strong and unnervingly quiet and retiring, not at all what I had imagined a trained killer to be. With them and all their equipment aboard there was even less room than usual. Their kit was stowed in the torpedo compartment and consisted of a variety of small arms, explosives, diving gear and two different types of boat, the buzzard and the canoe. When using the canoe or the buzzard, both of which were inflatable, the SBS would remain in the torpedo compartment. The submarine would be brought to the surface using only the hydroplanes. This meant that she was still negative buoyant and ready to dip beneath the waves at the slightest hint of danger. Once the torpedo loading hatch was clear of the water it was opened and Boots Capper, the leading torpedoman, and myself, dressed in diving suits would step out into the well around the hatch. Standing there, waist deep in water, with the sea only a few inches from the open hatch, we would be passed all the SBS equipment. Their boats, either the canoe or buzzard, would then be inflated using high pressure air in bottles attached to them and then, the last thing to come out of the boat was the SBS troops themselves. They would climb into their boats while Boots and I leapt back through the hatch and shut it behind us. Once they were ready in their boats the submarine would just sink beneath the water and leave the SBS floating on the surface, ready to paddle into shore and wipe out an entire third world country, or whatever it was they were supposed to do.

We had practised this, a number of times over the past few days, and it was becoming routine. We began another run. The boat planed to the surface and Boots and I scrambled out of the hatch and prepared to receive the gear from the guys below. No sooner had we stepped out than the boat began to dive beneath us. We turned to jump back down the hatch but, already, the water was over the lip and pouring into the boat. The lads inside did exactly the right thing: they shut the hatch. The only trouble was that Boots and I were still outside. The boat sank below us and we both struggled out of the hatch well. If either one of us had managed to get caught up in any one of the numerous obstructions we would have been dragged down with the boat and drowned. Panic adds an awful lot of strength to endeavour you know. Boots and I managed to swim clear of the hatch well and, as the boat slid beneath the surface, we began to tread water. Now, here was a predicament. It was about two o'clock in the morning, we were in the middle of the Mediterranean Sea and we were without boat. Boots gracefully turned around in the water to face me. The phosphorescence in the water cast a strange green glow over us every time we moved and caused the water to ripple or break. Boots looked straight into my eyes and, without a hint of a smile said,

"Right Chas, which way's Gibraltar?"

"How the hell should I know?" I retorted. I was too busy trying to keep my self afloat to worry about our next run ashore. After all, we had no lifejackets. We had only been in the water for a few minutes and I was knackered already. I really would have to give up smoking.

"Come on Chas, we've got to swim somewhere, we can't just tread water till we drown."

"Boots. What makes you think I know where Gibraltar is for God's sake?" I said, coughing as I swallowed a goodly dose of salt water.

"Well, you're the one who does navigation, not me." He said.

I tried to think. How far out of Gibraltar would we have been when I last looked at the chart. It must have been at least a hundred miles. I'd only ever got my four hundred yards swimming badge. As we trod water in silence, trying to think what to do, we heard a rush of water. A bright burst of phosphorescence broke the surface of the sea some distance away. There was the unmistakeable sound of diesel engines coughing into life and shouts as the submarine surfaced and the bridge was manned. Slowly the boat made its way toward us, crew on the casing with torches searching the water. We shouted back and, after what seemed an age we were unceremoniously hauled back onboard.

The following morning Boots and I submitted a request form each asking to be granted two weeks survivors leave, a reasonable request under the circumstances I felt. The Captain refused the request and countered it with an allegation that the pair of us had left the boat without permission and were therefore guilty of being Absent Without Leave. We called it quits.

CHAPTER TWENTY-FIVE

On the way back from the Med Onslaught was scheduled to visit Oporto in Portugal. It was a fairly popular run ashore and the crew were looking forward to some fun in the sun.

Mick and I were already trying to come up with another ruse and, to be honest, we were struggling to come up with something new. Then, I saw it, there in black and white, a section of Queen's Regulations for the Royal Navy that, I was sure, would have been long since forgotten. I showed it to Mick and we decided to go ahead and use it to get one over on, of all people, the Captain.

Requestman's table was due to be held in the next few days to promote those that had passed exams and award good conduct badges to those men that had managed another four years of undetected crime. Mick and I went to see the Coxswain and handed him our request forms. He gave them a quick glance and threw them in the appropriate paperwork tray in his small office. Then he stopped what he was doing, looked at us and pulled them back out of the tray. His mouth opened visibly as he read them, properly.

"You have got to be joking. Haven't you?" he said looking in our direction with a look of incredulity on his face.

"No Coxswain, I think you'll find that those requests are perfectly in order." I said.

"But you can't do that, can you?"

"I think you will find we can 'Swain." Said Mick, and we turned and walked away, back to the Forends to plan our strategy.

On the day of the Captain's table Mick and I were waiting outside the wardroom. All the other requestmen were called in before us which was unusual. Normally you were called in strict order of seniority and, as Mick and I were going in together, we should have been in first. Still, all this waiting just added to the spice as far as we were concerned. Finally it was just us left.

The Coxswain's voice rang out from the wardroom.

"Chief Petty Officer Harrow and Petty Officer Cooke."

"Sir." We shouted together and in we marched, faced the Captain and saluted. He saluted back and leant forward on the small lectern that had been placed on the wardroom table.

"Sir," began the Coxswain, "a joint request by Chief Petty Officer Harrow and Petty Officer Cooke."

"Very well Coxswain, read out the request." Said the Captain looking slightly puzzled. A complaint by two men together in the Royal Navy is classed as mutiny, still punishable by death. A request by two men together, although not mutiny, was still an extremely unusual event.

"Aye aye sir. Chief Petty Officer Harrow and Petty Officer Cooke, request by both men for permission to grow a pigtail." Said the Coxswain, and took a deep breath.

The Captain took one look at us across the lectern and made his decision.

"Request denied, march the men out Coxswain."

"Excuse me sir," I said, "if I may be allowed to speak in favour of the request."

The Captains eyebrows did a little dance before settling in a frown across his forehead. He leant forward further.

"Well, carry on TI, I can't wait to hear what you two jokers have to say now."

"Thank you sir." I continued. "According to Queens Regulations sir, and I quote, 'Any rating or man desirous of the growing of a pigtail must be permitted to do so. Any man growing such a pigtail will be entitled to the issue of beeswax with which to hold the hair in place. A minimum of two men must request to grow the hair thus, so as to allow the rendering of plaits one upon the other.' Basically sir, you cannot deny us permission to grow our pigtails and the Navy has to supply us with beeswax to put on them. Chief Harrow and I constitute two ratings and we can therefore plait each others hair to keep it tidy. I don't like to present you with a fait accompli but, I'm afraid you must grant our request."

The Captain stood up straight and scratched the hair behind his ear.

"I need a few moments to check the regulations on this one you two, therefore I will stand you over for ten miutes while the Coxswain and I check out the rules together. Stood over for ten minutes, Coxswain, march them out."

"Stood over for ten minutes. Salute the Captain. About turn, quick march. Wait outside and we'll call you back in as soon as we have a decision."

Mick and I went out into the passageway and stood there giggling and cackling. We'd done it. We had caught the old man on the hop and we were going to be the longest haired men in the navy. Who knows, we could even rope the rest of the crew in on this and start a plague of pigtails, and there was nothing the skipper could do about it.

It only took five minutes for the regulations to be checked. We had done our homework and we knew we were on firm ground. We went through the rigmarole once more of marching in, saluting and the request being read out to the Captain.

"Gentlemen, you are absolutely right." Said the skipper. "I am not allowed to prevent you from growing your pigtails, I must therefore, and against my better judgement, grant your request. Coxswain, request granted, march them out."

Once again we saluted the captain and, with huge grins on our faces marched toward the door.

"Just one thing before you go gents."

We turned round and looked at the Captain. He was grinning. What was he up to?

"Are you looking forward to your run ashore in Oporto?"

"Yes sir." Said Mick.

"Very much so sir." I said, returning his smile.

"And I gather you have been given your subsistence, quite a tidy sum of escudos I should think, is that right?"

"Yes sir." I replied.

"Then you won't mind if the supply officer comes with you to your mess and takes those Escudos back then will you?"

"I don't understand sir. Why would he want our money back?" asked Mick.

"Well, you see chaps, you were right about my not being able to prevent you growing a pigtail, however, in your haste to make a complete arse of me, I think you may have stopped reading a little too prematurely. You see, the next section states that men permitted to grow a pigtail, in order to maintain good order and naval discipline, may not proceed ashore from their ship until a minimum of two plaits can be woven into the hair. So, as you will not be allowed ashore in Portugal, you will not therefore be needing the money paid to you for subsistence purposes. What is more, I am sure that, as you are not permitted to leave the boat you will of course be allowing those senior rates, who were designated for duty during the period, to remain ashore whilst you carry out the duty for them. That is all, enjoy the next week or so on the boat. Thank you gents." And with that he began to sort his paperwork and conclude the requestmen's table.

"Sir, before we go," said Mick, a look of panic on his face, "Petty Officer Cooke and I would like to revise our original request and now submit a request to carry on cutting our hair."

The Captain looked down his nose at us.

"Request denied, dismissed." And with that he turned and walked out of the wardroom. Mick and I nearly came to blows there and then. Whose stupid idea was it to try it on with the skipper anyway? Five minutes later the supply officer was taking back our money and the Coxswain was rewriting the duty roster for the week in Oporto. Mick and I were now duty every day. This time the wind up had backfired and we were not happy bunnies.

The whole crew must have been in on the reversed wind up because all week we were thanked profusely by the other senior rates for volunteering to do their duties for them. The Captain kept it going right up until the morning we pulled alongside in Portugal. Only then did he relent and let us ashore. I would never try and get one over on a skipper again. Well, not unless a really good opportunity presented itself and, even then, I'd make sure I researched the windup properly.

I thoroughly enjoyed my run ashore in Oporto but, by now I was looking forward to getting home and seeing Caroline and the boys once more. The boat made the transit back to the UK on the surface and, for once the Bay of Biscay was flat calm. We made good time and, before long, we were making our way up the channel toward home.

It was our last night at sea and I was taking a walk around the boat, checking both the forward and after torpedo compartments. In the after ends I was checking all the weapons stowages. My nose began to wrinkle, something smelt pretty foul. It wasn't unusual for some pretty nasty smells to build up in a submarine, especially in the after sections. When the control room was busy and the toilets out of use, or a watch keeper was required to stay in the same compartment for six hours, the accepted method of relief was to use an empty gallon detergent container to urinate into. It was emptied into the toilet at the first opportunity. After all, the men had to live in the space too. But this was something different, it was foul. I popped my head into the stoker's mess.

"Alright lads, sorry to bother you on Channel Night but has anyone noticed a horrible smell back here?"

There was a general shaking of heads.

"What sort of smell TI?" asked one man.

"Well, to be honest, it smells as though someone has crapped in the bilges." I said.

"Oh that. No, that's okay, it's Ginger's pet turd."

I was a bit taken aback by this and asked for an explanation which was duly forthcoming. One of the stoker's, we shall just call him Ginge, had come to Onslaught under a bit of a cloud. He had been a leading stoker on his previous boat but there had been a clash of personality between him and his Petty Officer. It resulted in a fist fight where Ginge had caught the unfortunate Petty Officer a right crack on the beak. The two of them were disciplined. Ginge, who was deemed to be most at fault, had been disrated to MEM1 while the Petty Officer had managed to keep his rank but had been drafted off the boat and sent to work in the oil analysis lab in the base. The Petty Officer's job involved receiving oil samples from every boat in the fleet and testing them for contamination. The samples, contained in test tubes were sent through the internal mail in padded envelopes. These envelopes were issued to every boat with a printed address label already stuck on the front. It would seem that Ginge was wreaking, or should that be reeking, his revenge on the unfortunate Petty Officer. Once a week he would take a padded envelope to the toilet and place a turd therein. This envelope he placed in his locker and the previous week's excrement, that had been festering in the locker for seven days, would be sent to the lab in the guise of an oil sample. The poor Petty Officer received about thirty envelopes each week and he knew that, each week, one of them would contain a turd, courtesy of Ginge. Not a pleasant thought and, for once, it could hardly be said that revenge is sweet!

CHAPTER TWENTY-SIX

I had been on Onslaught for almost eighteen months by now and she was another boat due a refit. We had been promised that submarines refitting would always be placed into the hands of the home dockyard, in our case Portsmouth. This suited me down to the ground as Caroline and I had, by now, bought our house in Gosport and we were well and truly settled. Gavin was at school and the twins were at playschool. Caroline had got herself a part time job and things were looking rosy. I suppose it was just too much to hope for that the Navy could leave us alone. As the date for the refit drew nearer everyone onboard was planning for the refit to take place in Portsmouth. And then the announcement was made. Onslaught was to refit in Plymouth. The news hit like a bombshell for me and I began to hope that I would be taken off of the boat and sent elsewhere. I really didn't fancy another extended period of living away from home. After all, they only left a skeleton crew on a refitting boat. I was sure things would turn out for the best. Oh, how wrong I was. My name appeared on the list of men remaining on the boat when it went to Plymouth and I had the prospect of another two and a half years away from the family, Caroline and the boys staying at home in Portsmouth while I lived in naval barracks in Plymouth. Still, there were a few months left before that happened so we vowed to make the best of things.

We were alongside HMS Dolphin. It was a three week maintenance period and essential repairs were being carried out in preparation for the next trip, a short three week hop around the Atlantic on various exercises.

"TI to the wardroom."

The tannoy in the mess interrupted my coffee and I reluctantly dragged myself along the passageway to officer country. I knocked and poked my head through the curtain.

"Morning TI." It was the torpedo officer.

"Morning sir, you wanted to see me?"

"Yes, just a quick one. This signal has just come in from squadron. They're going to weld up the after tubes in refit and there's a few bits and pieces to be done before we get there. I suppose now would be an ideal time to do it, if you would be so kind."

He handed me the flimsy signal paper and I went back to the mess to read it.

After coffee I went to the torpedo compartment to see the lads. They were sitting on the step inside the watertight door having a coffee and a chat.

"Morning lads, everything okay then?"

There was a general nodding so it seemed that my boys were happy enough.

"Look lads, you know we've been having problems with the after tubes for years and they've finally decided to do away with the old Mk20 torpedo and weld the tubes shut. When we're in refit they are going to seal the stern caps and blank off the inboard end. I've just got a signal here, we're not loading any more Mk20s so the afterends will have no weapons in it for the next trip. We've been ordered to scrap the after loading rails. Boots, here's the details. The scrap lorry will be down next Thursday to collect them so, closer to the day, if you and the lads can get the rails out of the lay apart store and get them onto the lorry for me?"

I was assured that this would not be a problem.

I had been having a few problems with an old elbow injury and I had been scheduled to have an operation in the Naval Hospital at Haslar. I would be going in on the Wednesday and coming out on the Friday. I would be away for the scrapping of the after torpedo loading rails but I wasn't worried. They were a good set of lads and Boots was a good leading hand. I spoke to Boots the day before I went into hospital to make sure he knew what was needed while I was away. The maintenance was ticking along nicely and we were looking forward to going back to sea for a bit.

My operation went well and I was back on the boat the following Monday. We were due to sail on the Thursday and we were scheduled to load weapons on the Tuesday, a full outfit of twenty two torpedoes. It was hard work for the torpedomen as manhandling a ton and a half of metal containing half a ton of explosives is no easy task. Perhaps it may help the reader if I explain how a torpedo is loaded into a submarine. Each boat has a set of specially made rails, one set each for the after and forward torpedo compartments. These rails are bolted to the casing on the outside and hang from brackets on the deckhead inside the boat. These rails are rigged the day before the load. On the morning of the load the torpedo loading hatch is opened and another, short section of rails is added to bridge the gap between outside and inside. The torpedo arrives on a lorry and a broad steel band is placed around it. A crane is then attached to the torpedo and, hanging nose down, it is lowered onto the rails. On the band is a set of wheels which fit into the rails to allow it to be lowered carefully into the boat. A rope is attached to the nose ring of the weapon and, as the crane lowers away, the lads in the boat haul on the rope to keep the torpedo at the right angle. Once inside the boat a hydraulic press, or winch, is attached to the weapon and the crane hook is disconnected. The torpedo is then lifted off of the rails onto trolleys sitting on heavy steel beams inside the boat and is then pushed and pulled, by hand, into the correct position. Some of the weapons are loaded straight into the tubes to make room for those coming behind. The whole process lasts all day and the men are exhausted at the end of it. The rails that the torpedo sits on during the process are individually made for each boat and are made when the boat is built.

Monday was spent preparing for the load and at the end of the day I went home having ensured that the inner and outer rails were rigged and the duty torpedoman was detailed off to fit the bridging section, or intermediates as they are properly called, in the early hours of the morning. We were just about ready.

Tuesday came and I was up early. I went straight to the boat and crossed the gangway. The intermediate rails weren't rigged and I was a bit annoyed that it hadn't been done. Still, I was sure they were in the process of doing it. I took the red flag to the bridge and hoisted it up the short flag pole. It signified that we were transferring explosives. I made my way to the Forends where I found Boots, the leading torpedoman and Shuffs, one of the lads, in deep conversation.

"Alright then Boots, nearly ready to go?" I asked. I looked around the forends and saw that all the necessary equipment was neatly laid out ready to go. All the non essential items had been stowed. Things looked good.

"There's a bit of a problem TI." Said Boots, looking at his feet.

"Well, not to worry, we'll get it sorted before the ammo lorry arrives." I said, trying to sound upbeat and optimistic. "What's the matter then, crane driver overslept?"

"We've lost the loading rails."

My heart skipped a dozen beats and I looked between the two to see if this was one of their wind ups.

"What do you mean we've lost the loading rails? How can you lose two lumps of metal that weigh about three hundred pounds the pair? Have you checked the lay apart store?"

"Yep. All we can find are the intermediate rails for the after torpedo compartment."

"No, you must have made a mistake, you scrapped the after loading rails last wee…"

I looked at Boots who shuffled his feet and went red.

"Boots. Please tell me you checked and double checked those rails before you put them on the scrap lorry."

There was an ominous silence as he inspected the deck plates still further.

"I'm sorry TI. I just put the first ones I found on the scrap lorry, I never thought to look and make sure they were the after ones."

This was a crisis. We had twenty two weapons arriving in an hour, we were sailing in a couple of days and we had to have those weapons on the boat but we had no way of getting them on.

"You prat. Okay, Shuffs, go and measure the fittings for the rails and then go round all the other boats and see if theirs will fit us. Boots and I will go and visit the torpedo officer, won't we Boots?"

"Yes TI."

We split up, Shuffs went off with a tape measure while Boots and I tried to explain the problem to our illustrious leader. He was not happy. I tried to reassure him that Shuffs was bound to find a set that would fit somewhere in the fleet. I felt a lot less optimistic than I sounded. I was right too. Shuffs returned within half an hour. We were out of luck. He'd managed to get nothing except a fair amount of mickey taking. I sent Boots back to the forends to make sure everything else was ready and the Torpedo Officer and I went to see the Captain. He was most annoyed. I think I was off his Christmas card list.

"So TI. What do we do now?" Asked the skipper.

"Well sir, it's never been done before but, if the crane driver is willing to give it a go, we'll try and get them on without the rails in place. It's going to be bloody hard work and I don't even know whether it's possible, but, we've got to give it a go."

Word had spread around the other boats like wildfire. The first torpedo came off the lorry in front of a huge crowd on the jetty. They wanted to watch this, a submarine first. There was a general racket of jeers and abuse. It just made us even more determined to do it and prove them all wrong. They were running a book on whether we would be able to do it.

The lads worked like Trojans. They were sweating and knackered after the first weapon had been loaded. It wasn't easy and I have never worked so hard in my life but, the crowd slowly diminished until there were just a few interested onlookers. Even they seemed to have a grudging admiration for the fact that we were managing to load the weapons against all the odds. We finished the load at eleven o'clock that evening, tired but victorious. I bought the lads several crates of beer and we had a muted celebration. It wasn't to be the end of the matter. It was the last load before refit so we wouldn't have to go through it again but firstly they had to come off before went into refit and secondly, somebody at squadron headquarters had heard about it and was baying for blood, my blood.

The last night alongside and I had been clobbered to do duty senior rate. JJ, the most junior officer onboard was the duty Grunter. It was normal for the duty officer and the duty senior rate to get together in either the senior rates mess or the wardroom for a drink at some time during the duty. It was difficult sitting in a mess alone so the rules were quite relaxed. I had invited JJ in for a beer and we were chatting about life and putting the world to rights. JJ came from a very well to do family and, it was rumoured, was somewhere toward the bottom of the list for succession to the British throne. He was a bit of a black sheep as all his ancestors had joined the army, as far back as the days of The Duke of Wellington. JJ had broken that tradition and had put his family on the right tracks by joining the Navy. We got round to houses and I told JJ that I had recently bought my own home in Portsmouth.

"Really TI, and how much was that?" he asked in his normal silver spoon voice.

"It cost me fifteen and a half thousand pound s, not too bad I suppose."

"Jolly well done TI, I've just purchased a small property in Fulham, sixty thousand pounds."

"Blimey, what's the mortgage on that then?"

He looked at me puzzled.

"What's a mortgage TI?"

We lived in different worlds.

The subject moved on to gardens and gardening. I was quite proud of my little patch of England and did my best to keep the roses smelling sweet and the vegetables grown there tasting good.

"Yes, my parents have a little garden at their place, about sixty acres I think, just a small plot really."

Sixty acres, that was bigger than the entire housing estate on which I lived.

"Who looks after that then sir?" I asked.

"Well, Daddy employs several gardeners, Oh and we do have a retired naval commander in twice a week to cut the grass. Rather handy really, if I have a bad week at sea I just go home and give the commander a damned good bollocking, makes me feel so much better."

The image of JJ a slim sub lieutenant of about twenty two tearing a strip off the commander in the garden brought a smile to my face. Poor old JJ, he was a prime target for the crew. He was so naïve.

The following morning we slipped and proceeded to sea. I had all but forgotten about the loading rails incident and soon settled into the routine of watchkeeping. We had been at sea for about ten days. It was night and the boat was in semi darkness. Those not on watch were in bed asleep and, having just been relieved from my position in the control room, I decided to have a cup of tea in the mess. I stepped through the curtain covering the doorway and reached out with my left hand to take one of the communal tea mugs from the rack on the wall. I stopped in my tracks. There, with his trousers and pants round his ankles, was Les Bryant, one of the electrical artificers. He was holding a mess mug in his right hand. In his left was clutched his penis which was dangling into the mug which appeared to be half full of some liquid.

"What the hell are you doing Les? You've got your knob in a mug."

"Sssshhh." He hissed. "You'll wake someone up."

"Never mind that Les, would you like to tell me why your dangling your bell end in one of the mess mugs?"

"I've got a bit of a dose of the clap, Chas. I'm on the old tablets and I've got to rinse me dick in this solution once a day. I couldn't think what else to use."

Even I was aghast at this. Here was a man bearing a sexually transmitted disease and he was washing his weeping parts in the mess tea mugs.

"Jesus Les, that's disgusting. Surely you could have found something else." I turned to pick up a mug from the rack. "Look, just let me know which one you've used and then, for God's sake keep it in your locker will you."

"The trouble is Chas, I've used a different one each day. I think. I've just been grabbing a mug out the rack and getting on with the treatment."

I threw him a disgusted look. Discretion being the better part of valour I decided to give the tea a miss, well at least until I could find a mug of my own and lock it away for my sole use.

The exercise over, Onslaught made her way back to Portsmouth. We entered the shipping channels leading into Portsmouth Harbour and it became busy in the control room. It was late evening and it was dark outside. The boat was at river routine and I was on the navigation plot. JJ was on the periscope taking bearings on fixed points ashore and I was transferring the bearings onto the chart and working out our position. This information was then passed to the officer of the Watch on the bridge along with advice on which course to steer to ensure that we either remained on track or regained it if we had wandered slightly off course. The fixes were being called every three minutes and I was working hard to keep up.

"Light, white flashing once every three seconds bears that. 265." Called JJ.

I looked on the chart and there roughly where it should have been was the light marked on the chart. I plotted the bearing along with the other two he had given me. We were slightly to starboard of track and I recommended that we came slightly to port to regain our original course. Another fix was on its way.

"Same white light bears that. 278."

Again I plotted the fix. We were even farther to starboard than the last time.

"Fix again sir, bad fix." I called to JJ.

He harrumphed and swung the periscope around.

"White light bears that. 281. Right hand edge Isle of Wight bears that. 324. and right hand edge of fort bears that. 032."

I plotted the fix. Even farther to starboard.

"Are you sure of those points sir? it puts us three cables to starboard of track and moving out of the lanes." I called. I was beginning to worry now.

"Yes TI that's a good fix, pass it to the bridge."

I reported to the Officer of the Watch and suggested a further alteration of course to port. Onslaught came left to take up its new heading.

"Sir, I'm not happy about this, that fix doesn't seem right. Are you sure we're looking at the right light?"

JJ strolled across to the plotting table and I showed him the light I had been using to plot his fixes.

"That's the one TI, definitely the right one. Don't worry, I've got it all under control."

"FULL ASTERN TOGETHER, STARBOARD THIRTY, STANDBY COLLISION FORRARD." The officer of the watch's voice had an element of panic to it. I leapt across the control room and hit the general alarm. I made the emergency broadcast.

"Shut bulkhead doors. Standby collision forrard. Emergency stations emergency stations, shut bulkhead doors, standby collision forrard."

The boat was shaking as both propellers went full astern. The Captain came flying into the control room and up to the bridge.

Slowly the boat came to a halt in the water and, after a short delay the captain came storming down the ladder into the control room. He flew across to the chart table and looked at the plot.

"TI, what the bloody hell are you doing. That white light you've been fixing on doesn't exist. We damned nearly ran aground."

I was lost for words but luckily JJ was a real gentleman.

"Excuse me captain, it's not the TI's fault. It's mine. He did question that fixing point and I assured him that it was right. If anyone to blame it is me. The TI is not to blame in any way."

The Captain gave JJ a right royal roasting there and then, in front of the entire control room watch. It could be heard throughout the boat. He stormed out of the control room leaving JJ looking sheepish and downcast.

"Sorry about that TI. My fault. Should have listened."

The chart was inspected closely by the navigating officer and the first lieutenant. The only explanation they could come up with was that JJ had been fixing on a motorcycle going along the coast road. The flashing light was its headlight appearing and disappearing behind the trees and obstacles on the side of the road. JJ was quiet and miserable for the remainder of the short trip into harbour and alongside the trots at HMS Dolphin.

Once alongside the duty watch took over the boat and the rest of us disappeared off toward home, myself and JJ included. After a couple of days off it was back to work and, as luck would have it, JJ and I were duty again the following Saturday, Easter weekend. Again JJ and I spent a pleasant evening sitting and chatting. I noticed that JJ had very quickly got over the fiasco with the navigation and I felt obliged to ask him about it.

"I must say sir, despite the other nights little faux pas, you look pretty happy. Very happy in fact."

"Do you know TI, I am, I had a very good couple of days off."

"I'm glad to hear it sir." I replied, genuinely pleased for him. After all, despite being an officer, he was just a nice guy.

"Yes TI, I had a very good few days."

I looked at him and he smiled.

"I sacked the bloody commander." He said and went back to his pint.

The following morning I went to see JJ in the wardroom. It was Easter Sunday and the new duty watch were ready to take over. I asked for his permission to allow the Saturday's duty watch to be dismissed and spend Easter with their families.

"In just a few moments, TI. Just one small thing to do." And with that he picked up the microphone and made a broadcast throughout the boat.

"Do you hear there, Saturday's and Sunday's duty watch, muster in the wardroom to celebrate the resurrection of our Lord, Jesus Christ."

I visibly winced. The lads would kill him. Already I could hear them clattering along the passageways toward us. The last thing they wanted was a compulsory church service.

"Come in gentlemen and take a seat, please." Said JJ to the gathering throng of angry sailors.

There was a shuffling and everybody found a seat. They did not look happy.

JJ turned to a small cupboard behind him and opened the door. It was the wardroom bar. He pulled out a variety of bottles containing a selection of spirits, and a handful of glasses.

"Okay then chaps. Who's having what?"

The mood lightened considerably as JJ played mine host and served everyone with a full glass of the spirit of their choice. He was slopping brandy and whisky all over the table as he struggled to keep up with demand.

"Sir," I said, "this is very good of you but, well, to be honest, you're not very good at this serving lark, are you?"

"Ti, I must be honest and agree, you see, normally, my butler does it." He replied with a smile. "Cheers."

I finished my drink with a grin. I was right, he was a bloody nice chap.

CHAPTER TWENTY-SEVEN

It wasn't long before Onslaught went into refit in Plymouth. Once again I was separated from the family and living in barracks. What made it worse this time was that I was the only senior rate on the boat who hadn't moved his family down to the West Country. I was alone in a mess full of skimmers and they did not like submariners. There were a few junior rates living in barracks initially, but they soon clubbed together and rented flats around the area. I was alone in the barracks and I was thoroughly fed up. To make matters worse, the subject of the torpedo loading rails had raised its ugly head again. I was called into a meeting with the Captain and the Torpedo Officer. They explained to me that, even though I had been incapacitated and in hospital at the time that the mistake was made, I was ultimately responsible for the error. The Captain assured me that, as far as he was concerned, it was a minor matter and it was only being pursued because someone at squadron headquarters had decided that somebody had to carry the can. Between them they assured me that I was not to worry, it was a little thing that would soon go away.

A few weeks passed and I began to believe that it had been forgotten. The Torpedo Officer had left the boat and the Captain was due to be relieved very shortly. Then the Coxswain called me to his office and told me that I was to attend Captain's Table as a defaulter the following morning. My heart sank, but I still felt that this was a storm in a teacup. I duly reported the following morning and was called into the room. The Captain was leaning on the lectern and was looking serious.

"TI, I'm afraid things have become a little messy." He said.

I looked at the Coxswain who quickly looked away. He knew something I didn't.

It would appear that squadron have really got their teeth into this in a big way. I have been ordered to charge you with neglect of duty. Coxswain, please read the charge."

The Coxswain looked anywhere except me as he read out the relevant acts and sections of the Naval Discipline Regulations. The Captain spoke again.

"TI, this is a serious charge. Your divisional officer has recently left this boat, however, I have here a written reference as to the excellent nature of your character whilst serving in Onslaught. I now have to offer you a choice of hearing. You may elect for your case to be heard at a Naval Courts Martial, in which case a date will be set by the relevant authorities, or you may elect to have your case heard by me and to accept any punishment which I may feel to be justified. Now don't be a complete turd and go for the first one. If you select me I'll see you alright."

I looked at him astounded. I'd never heard anything like this before in my life. Here was the Captain treating me like an old school tie buddy.

I was marched out and the Coxswain followed me into our mess. He sat next to me and brought me coffee. He explained that he had only found out about the court martial a minute before I was called in.

"What would you do then?" I asked. I think I had already decided that I would rather take my punishment from somebody that I knew. A court martial would be a bit of a lottery.

"Chas, if you elect captain's punishment and plead guilty, he'll see you alright. I know he will. That's what I'd do."

A week later I was back in front of the Captain. I informed him that

I would rather my case was heard by him. I was stood over for ten minutes while the Captain read through the evidence from both sides. I was called back in. The Captain looked at the Coxswain who had a face like a poker.

He began.

"Sir, Petty Officer Weapons Engineering Mechanic Cooke. He is charged with neglect of duty in that he did permit torpedo loading rails, an essential item of ship's equipment, to be destroyed."

"Thank you Coxswain. Petty Officer Cooke, you have elected to have your case heard by me and to accept my punishment. Is that still the case?"

"Yes sir." I said, looking him in the eye.

"Very well. I have read evidence both for the prosecution and the defence. I would like to hear one more person's opinion in this matter. Coxswain."

I looked round wondering what on earth the Coxswain had to do with this.

"Sir," he began, "in my opinion Petty Officer Cooke is a highly skilled and efficient Torpedo Instructor, he has worked hard whilst a crewmember on Onslaught and has become highly proficient in all the duties he has been asked to perform."

I looked at him, he was playing a blinder. How could I be punished too severely after such a glowing testimony? He continued.

"It is for this reason that I feel that this lapse into crass stupidity should be punished by the award of a penalty so severe as to deter future misbehaviour by this rating or any other. It is my opinion that, hanging and flogging having been abolished, this rating should serve a lengthy term of imprisonment. He should be reduced in rank to the minimum level permissible and, on completion of the prison sentence, be dishonourably discharged from the service. In short sir, this Petty Officer is a disgrace to the uniform he wears and the ship upon whose books he is currently borne for duty."

My legs nearly collapsed. I was struggling for breath. The two of them had stitched me up a treat. I very nearly lunged at the Coxswain and strangled him. The Captain broke my concentration.

"Petty Officer Cooke, I have heard the Coxswain's views on this affair and I think he's talking a complete load of arse. I think this whole affair has been blown out of all proportion and I therefore intend to punish you by means of a reprimand. Dismissed."

The orders were given for me to on caps, about turn and march out. I was so stunned by the events that had just occurred that I followed the orders automatically. I was half way to the door when the Captain and the Coxswain could contain themselves no longer. They fell about the room laughing and congratulating each other on the performance. I had been well and truly had. The bait had been thrown and I had swallowed it hook line and sinker. I turned around in the doorway.

"Oh very good. Congratulations the pair of you. Okay. You won, I fell for it."

The Captain stopped laughing long enough to look me in the eye.

"TI, I had to get you back for that one about the pigtail." He said and resumed the laughter. As I walked out of the door I was left with an image of the Captain and the Coxswain, tears rolling down their faces, clapping each other on the back. I had finally got my come uppance.

Some months later I was being interviewed by the Electrical Officer as part of my annual appraisal and curiosity got the better of me.

"Sir, can I see that reprimand on my papers? I've never seen one before."

"Well you won't see one now either, we didn't bother putting it on. Reprimands are taken off your papers before you leave the boat anyway. It just wasn't worth the hassle TI."

A year had passed since Onslaught had entered refit and I was the proud recipient of another draft chit. It had been decided that, with a year and a half of the refit still to go, and with a shortage of submariners in the fleet, my services in Plymouth could be dispensed with. I was on my way back to Portsmouth to join Oberon, the oldest diesel boat still in the fleet. I had been in the navy for thirteen and a half years, just over and I was missing my family. Caroline had spent the best part of our married life without me at home. She had worked hard and done a wonderful job of bringing up our three boys, virtually on her own but the strain was beginning to tell on us both. I had had enough of coming home and having my own children hide from me because they didn't know who I was. That really hurt and, despite the tough exterior, it was things like that which had worn me down over the years. Caroline and I had discussed the possibility of me leaving and finding a job out in the big wide world. Civvy Street was a frightening thought. I compared it to leaving prison. I had become institutionalised and I didn't want to leave, only to return six months or a year later.

The decision was made for me really. Before joining Oberon I was to spend a few months in Spare Crew. All that meant was that, if another TI went sick then I had to be ready to fly anywhere in the world at the drop of a hat and take his place. I said goodbye to the few men left on Onslaught and set off for Portsmouth once again. I had enjoyed some good times on her but the boat had lost her personality in refit. She was just a metal tube waiting to be filled and most of the crew I had been at sea with had left and moved on too. It was still a sad moment but at least I was going home.

I had the weekend off before reporting to Dolphin Spare Crew Office. I was detailed to work in the Small Afloat Workshops on the jetty pending anyone falling ill and I settled in to a fairly relaxed routine. I had been there about two weeks when I received a phone call. I was sent to sea that same day on Opportune for a three week patrol. I managed to make avery quick phone call to Caroline and let her know what had happened and I was off. Three weeks later and I finally got home again. I walked into the house. Caroline was at work and I had not yet managed to let her know I was coming home. I settled down in a chair with a cup of tea. The phone rang and I answered it.

"Chas, is that you?"

I thought I recognised the voice of the Spare Crew Warrant Officer.

"Yeah, is that you Mick?"

"Bad news I'm afraid. You've got another trip, we need you back in here now. It's urgent, sorry."

"But Mick," I pleaded, "I've only just this minute got back, surely there must be someone else who can do this trip. I haven't even seen the wife yet."

"Sorry Chas. If there was anyone else available I would have sent them but, you're it I'm afraid. See you in half an hour or so?"

There was a click as he hung up. I tried to get through to Caroline at work but the line was permanently engaged. I left her a note.

'Hello Darling. Goodbye Darling, been home been called, been shafted. I'll be a bit late home—about four weeks I think. Love you.'

I picked up my bag, still packed from the last trip and went straight back to the base. Mick explained what had happened. They had received a signal asking for a TI due to illness. Of all people, the TI on the Onyx, my mate Phil Makin had been taken ill. I tried another phone call to Caroline but it was still engaged and I was on my way without speaking to her. Car to Heathrow, British Airways Shuttle flight to Glasgow, car to Faslane and then a Bedford ten ton truck from there to the Kyles of Lochalsh, right up by the Isle of Skye. By the time I reached the Kyles I had been travelling almost eighteen hours. The Onyx was tied up to a buoy in the middle of the channel between the Isle and the mainland and a launch was waiting to take me out to her.

As we approached I could see the casing party releasing the buoy and the diesels were running. No sooner had I stepped onto the casing than we were slipped and under way. The boat was closed up at harbour stations and river routine. I went to the senior rates mess and made myself a cup of tea. I was determined to have a rest after my trip. About an hour later the crew fell out from harbour stations and went to patrol routine, river routine. I left the mess and went through the junior rates mess into the torpedo compartment. I stopped dead in my tracks, there sitting on the step, a steaming mug of coffee in his hands was Phil. He looked up at me in surprise.

"Chas, what the bloody hell are you doing onboard?" He asked, nearly choking on his coffee.

"More to the point Phil, what are you doing here?" I retorted.

"Chas, I'm the TI, you know that."

"Yeah, and so am I for this trip, or so spare crew told me."

"Hang on a minute Chas, have you come from spare crew in Dolphin."

"Yeah, we were told you were ill and they wanted a TI."

"Did it actually say that I was ill?" Asked Phil.

"I tried to picture the signal from drafty to the spare crew office.

"Now you mention it, no, it didn't. It said crew illness."

"That explains it mate. One of my able seamen has gone ill and was taken off yesterday. We asked for a replacement for him. I think we'd better go and see the Jimmy and find out what's going on.

A long discussion took place over several hours between me, Phil, the Electrical Officer, the Captain and the drafting office in Portsmouth by way of signal. It turned out that there was such a shortage of submariners that there wasn't a single able or leading seaman available in the fleet to take the place of the sick man. They had decided that, despite the fact that I had been a Petty Officer for seven years, I would take the place of the able seaman. So, for the next four weeks I carried out the duties of someone two ranks lower than me. I slept in the junior rates mess, ate with the junior rates and lost all my privileges as a senior rate. Don't get me wrong, I had no objection in reality with mixing in with the lads in the junior rates mess. They were a good bunch of lads but, rules are rules, and drafty had broken every rule in the book. I spoke to the Captain who advised me to state a complaint. I duly did just that and he pushed the complaint on up the ladder. As soon as I got back to Dolphin I was going to see the Captain, First Sub Squadron. In the meantime I had a patrol to get on with. It was a four week patrol and, at the end of it, the boat was going into Rosyth for one night before sailing again, for a two week exercise in the Atlantic prior to returning home to Portsmouth.

The night before we were due alongside in Rosyth the skipper called me to his cabin. He thanked me for the work I had done during the patrol and he apologised for the loss of my privileges. He wished me well with the complaint and assured me that I would be the first man over the gangway when we got alongside. An hour later he called me back to his cabin and looked extremely embarrassed as he explained that the leading writer, the ships clerk, had become a father overnight. Drafty had signalled the Onyx, telling them to keep me as the writer for the two week exercise.

"I've tried to get them to send someone else but they insist you stay TI." He said apologetically.

"Well, there's a bit of a problem there I'm afraid sir. You see, a few years ago I lost the little finger of my right hand. That means I can't type the letter L. Every other letter, not a problem, but that L just won't happen for me sir. I'll do my best."

I phoned Caroline from the jetty at Rosyth as soon as we were tied up and explained the situation. She burst into tears. I had never heard her so upset before and I began to realise just how hard this was on her and the kids. The Navy had just made my mind up for me.

The two week exercise was over and we were tying up alongside Dolphin. The patrol records were immaculate. I had spent the entire two weeks typing and there wasn't a letter L to be seen anywhere. Onyx had been in the Atantic Ocean, West of Ireand and spent a considerable time operating with Nimrod Aircraft of the Roya Air Force before returning to HMS Dophin. I often wondered what the boffins at Northwood made of those records.

I poked my head out of the hatch, blinking in the sunlight. There was Caroline, waiting on the jetty for me. It was the first time in nine and a half years of marriage that she had come to meet a boat. I ran up the gangway and hugged her. She was crying and I wiped the tears from her eyes. That night I told her that I had had enough. I was going to leave. Underneath the relief I could see the anxiety. Would I get a job, how would we do as civvies? We would find out, wouldn't we?

The following day I was summoned to see the Captain of SM1. I explained my complaint to him and he fully agreed. He passed it on up the ladder.

Two weeks later and I found myself sitting in the office of Commodore Naval Drafting, HMS Centurion. I had explained my complaint to him.

"The problem is, Petty Officer Cooke, we are so short of men in the navy that decisions like the one that affected you are having to be made."

"I'm sure that's the case sir but, you cannot deny that, in making that decision, you as an organisation contravened the Queens Regulations for the Royal Navy and you broke all the rules in the Drafting Book of reference, a book that your department wrote and insists that everybody abides by. Yet you yourself failed to abide by those references."

"I cannot deny that is the case PO Cooke, but, given the same set of circumstances, I would have no doubt, and no hesitation in taking the same decisions again."

"Well, you're not doing it to me again sir." I handed him a request form.

"What's this?" He said, taking it from me.

"That, sir, is my request for premature voluntary release. I am handing in my notice." I got up, saluted and left his office.

By the time I got back to Dolphin news of my conversation had been received by the Spare Crew Office. I was summoned in and they tried to talk me out of my decision. I stuck by it and, that day I began to work my period of notice, all eighteen months of it. Now I had the problem of being sent to Oberon, going to sea and, at the same time trying to find a job to go to when I left. It wasn't easy. I was writing to companies and asking for jobs and the standard reply, roughly translated was

'Thank you for your interest but we don't know whether there will be a company in eighteen months, let alone a job. Please call again when you have a month remaining in the Navy.'

This didn't do me much good. I had to have a job when I left. I had a wife, three children and a mortgage to support. I needed to know that I could pay my way. In the meantime, it was back to sea and the old routine.

CHAPTER TWENTY-EIGHT

Oberon, like Onslaught, was the nominated sneaky boat. It carried out all of the patrols where information needed by the UK was gathered for intelligence purposes. It was fairly exciting at times but it did mean that there weren't that many runs ashore outside Europe.

The crew were worked hard on the patrols and there were often an extra six or seven men onboard, for their language skills, so it was a crowded boat at sea. Being the oldest boat in the diesel fleet it did have more than its fair share of mechanical problems but the crew worked like Trojans to keep the boat in working order. It wasn't always the big mechanical faults that caused the most problems, even the smallest defects could cause chaos. We had been at sea for two weeks and we were dived in area where to surface would have caused a diplomatic incident, need I say more? The Wrecker came into the control room and spoke to the Officer of the Watch.

"Sir, can you make a pipe for me please? Heads and bathrooms out of use, the soil pipe is blocked."

The soil pipe was the large bore pipe that carried the waste from all of the toilets down to the sewage tank. If the soil pipe blocked the toilets just overflowed and became unusable. It was the least popular task for the stokers, having to clear three days worth of human waste from the pipe.

The broadcast was made and the toilets were out of use: For the next two days. It was horrible. Men were having to use any receptacle they could find to defecate into and then it had to be stowed until the toilets were back in use. After the first twenty four hours the boat reeked, even to our desensitised noses. The pipe had been poked prodded and rodded. It seemed that the blockage was farther along the pipework and almost certainly in an area which was inaccessible, without dismantling half the boat anyway. The captain was now taking a personal interest in the matter, so to speak. It would be highly embarrassing to him should he have to call off the patrol and return to Portsmouth because the bogs couldn't be used. It didn't seem to matter what they did, nothing could shift the blockage. Extreme measures were called for. The Wrecker explained his plan to the Captain. It involved a sheet of cling film, a stoker and the air system. The plan was to isolate all the toilets, except one, from the sewage tank. The tank would then be pressurised and, hopefully, the blockage would be pushed back up the pipework until it reached the single point of exit left to it, number two trap, the centre toilet. That would be covered with a large sheet of clingfilm, of several layers thickness, to catch the offending blockage. The captain agreed that it was the only course of action remaining and gave his permission to carry on.

The clingfilm was placed over the top of the toilet pan, loosely so as to allow for expansion should the blockage be of a considerable size. The unfortunate stoker was selected. His job was to watch the clingfilm and signal the arrival of the blockage when it was blown clear. The wrecker lined up the system to blow the tank overboard but, in order to allow the pressure to build up, he ensured that the hull valve, which normally allowed the sewage to flow out into the sea, remained firmly shut. The air pressure was slowly increased in the tank. The stoker and the Wrecker were using small portable battery operated phones to communicate. A prearranged signal had been agreed to signal the clearance of the blockage which would necessitate the Wrecker shutting off the air to the tank and immediately venting the pressure. The air began to enter the sewage tank. There was a muted sound of bubbling and gurgling but nothing at the business end. The stoker spoke to the Wrecker and told him that, as far as he could see, it was having no effect. A bit more air was called for. More pressure was put into the tank and again there was bubbling and gurgling, admittedly, this time, a little louder and it lasted a bit longer, but still no sign of the offending article or articles. A short conference took place and it was decided to go for broke. The Wrecker returned to his hole and the stoker to his toilet. The Wrecker really meant this one. He put a huge blast of air into the tank and kept it going. There was a huge rumbling and thundering sound. The stoker came hurtling out of the toilet and ran for it. Sensible man. That cling film is stretchy stuff. From the door of the toilet appeared a huge brown blister. It looked like a living organ. It was moving and swelling by the second. Eventually it could stretch no further. The Officer of the Watch was screaming into the microphone, urging the Wrecker to shut off the blow and vent the tank. It was too late. The cling film finally gave up and ruptured. Luckily it ruptured at the top and approximately ten pounds of congealed human waste, mixed with about three gallons of liquid from the same source burst forth like a fountain. Luckily, it went straight up in the air. Unluckily, the curve of the pressure hull deflected it and, still travelling at about twenty five miles per hour, the entire mess turned through ninety degrees and headed toward the starboard side of the boat. Luckily, again, there was only one radio operator in the wireless office directly opposite the toilet. Unfortunately for him he had the door open to keep the tiny space cool. The projectile hit him square in the back of the head. Its energy dissipated by the deflection and strike, that's where it stopped. It slowly oozed down the radio operator's back and splatters and ricochets slowly dripped from the equipment within the compartment. Not his lucky day really, but then, who cared? At last we could use the toilets. It was the first time since I joined diesel boats that I saw water coming from the single shower in the junior rate's bathroom. It was unfortunate that the poor victim had only one set of clothes with him. He spent the remainder of the patrol cleaning the wireless office dressed in borrowed clothing.

The toilets on a submarine are an endless source of amusement for the crew. They have come up with all sorts of tricks to play. Every crew member's family knows exactly how the toilet system works on the boat and the crew make sure that all visitors very quickly learn about the sewage tank. They seemed to get immense pleasure from telling visitors how members of the crew actually had to get inside the tank every so often in order to clean it. After all, we all know that shit sticks and, if too much sticks to the side of the tank, well, eventually it will be too small to get anything in it.

Every submarine has its fair share of social functions, most of which take the form of cocktail parties thrown by the senior rate's mess or the wardroom. A favourite trick was to commandeer a two way radio set. One radio would be retained by one of the crew while the other was hidden in amongst the pipework somewhere in the toilet. All that was needed then was for the unfortunate victim, usually a first time visitor to the boat, and always a female guest, who had been made aware of the toilet arrangements, to enter the selected toilet. The man with the radio would then wait patiently, allowing just enough time for the unfortunate lady to sort herself out and lower her clothing to the floor. One giveaway was the slight clank as the seat, under the weight of the victim, settled onto the stainless steel pan. The man with the radio would then shout into it, as loud as he could. 'Hey. Do you mind? I'm trying to work down here.' To the poor target of this prank the voice would appear to be coming from somewhere below her. There was generally a small crowd gathered by this time just waiting for the female to fly from the toilet with her clothes in disarray. It worked every time. One of the lads on Oberon had evolved this trick one stage further. He would wait for one of the guests, male or female, it didn't matter which to him, to use the toilet and, when he or she had finished he would check the relevant pan to determine whether the person had left a deposit, if you see what I mean. He would then don a polythene suit, complete with hood and rubber gloves and would then walk into the middle of the cocktail party, wearing the suit and with a fake dog turd, purchased from a local joke shop, on top of his head. At the top of his voice he would bring the cocktail party to a halt by demanding to know who had just used the toilet while he was cleaning the tank. It was a real showstopper and was always useful if guests seemed reluctant to end the celebrations. When you bear in mind that the guests were drinking and eating all night, and the cost of the food and drink had to be borne by all members of the mess, it did, over a period of time, save the crew a considerable amount of money.

I had three months left in the navy. I was sending begging letters to companies all over the UK in an attempt to find a job to go to. I was being singularly unsuccessful. Not a single job offer. I had my heart set on becoming a police officer and had even sent off to three different forces. I hadn't heard back from any of them as yet and I was beginning to panic. The phone rang one afternoon at home. I was on a weeks leave and had spent the entire time in a fruitless hunt for work. I was due back to work the next day. I was worried now, I had to find something soon or I might even be forced to withdraw my notice and stay in the Navy. Caroline answered the phone and handed it across.

"It's for you."

"Chas, it's the Coxswain. We've just had a phone call from squadron office, they want to see you first thing in the morning so you'd better go there before you come down the boat.

I replaced the receiver and looked at Caroline.

"What was that about then?" she asked.

"I haven't got a clue, they want me to go to squadron first thing in the morning. I haven't got the foggiest idea what they want."

The next morning, sharp at 0800, I was sitting in the office of the Commander who ran the squadron. I had been brought coffee and biscuits and he was smiling at me. I didn't like it one little bit.

"Okay then PO Cooke, I won't beat around the bush. You've done nearly fifteen years in the Navy, thirteen of those in submarines. We can't afford to lose any more men, we're short enough of experienced senior rates as it is. I want you to stay in. I want you to withdraw your request for release."

I looked at him. I had never been in this situation before.

"I'm sorry sir, I can't do that. I've spent the last fifteen months working toward leaving the Navy and making a go of civvy street. I need to spend some time with my family. I can't do that all the time I'm going to sea for eight months of every year. It's not fair to ask me now."

He looked at me and scratched his chin.

"If I could promise you two years of uninterrupted time with your family before I sent you back to sea again, would that allow you to reconsider?"

"Sir, I don't mean to sound cynical, but how are you going to get me two years at home with the family? You've just said yourself that the submarine service is short of experienced men. I'm bound to go to sea at some time in that two years, aren't I?"

"Not if I send you to Bermuda."

My jaw must have hit my knees. I couldn't think of anything to say. I just sat there like an idiot and gawped. He obviously saw that I was dumbstruck and decided to explain.

"There's a draft coming up in four weeks time for a ship's manager in Bermuda. It's a two year draft and is married accompanied, so you can take your family with you. It's probably the cushiest number in the Navy. All you have to do is live in Bermuda with your wife and kids. We supply you with a car and a house and, if you want it, we can even arrange for your wife to have a job out there. We pay for your kids schooling, you keep your submarine pay and you get local allowance, which will boost your pay considerably. You only work when a naval ship visits Bermuda and even then, all you have to do is arrange for local companies to supply the ship with all it needs. How about it then?"

I was actually sweating. I was so tempted to just take up a pen and sign on again. Instead I found myself saying.

"I need time to think about this sir. I'll have to discuss it with my wife. When do you need an answer?"

"Come and see me tomorrow morning, I have to know your decision by then. There's obviously a lot of people wanting this job. If I give it to you, I may lose you for two years but, when you come back, I'll get at least another five years out of you before you finish your twenty two. Talk it over with your family and I'll see you in the morning."

I walked out of his office in a daze. I went back to the boat and spoke to the Torpedo Officer about the offer. He, of course, being a young single officer, advised me to grab it with both hands. I began to imagine myself, sitting on a tropical sandy beach with Caroline beside me and the kids swimming in a turquoise sea. How could I turn it down?

Somehow I managed to get through the day and at four o'clock I drove home as fast as I could. I dashed into the house and through to the kitchen. Caroline was standing there leaning on the sink with a big smile on her face.

"This came for you this morning." She said, waving a large brown envelope.

I took it from her and saw the police crest on the front. I ripped it open. I was invited to attend a two day assessment for a police force in southern England. If successful I would almost certainly be offered a position with them when I left the Navy. I showed the letter to Caroline and she threw her arms round me.

I looked at her and she looked back.

"It's going to be alright, isn't it? We'll never have to be apart again." She said.

I made us both a cup of tea and sat in the living room reading the letter over and over. I came to a decision.

The following morning I saw the commander again. He was astounded when I thanked him for the offer but refused the draft to Bermuda. As I left he stood and shook my hand.

"You are determined to be with your family aren't you Cooke?"

"Yes I am. Goodbye sir."

CHAS COOKE JOINED THE POLICE ON DECEMBER 14TH 1987. HE IS STILL A SERVING POLICE CONSTABLE WITH THE FORCE AND HAS WORKED IN VARIOUS AREAS OF POLICE WORK. IN 1998 HE WAS SELECTED AS AN AIR OBSERVER, WITH THE POLICE AIR SUPPORT UNIT, AND CURRENTLY FLIES AS CREW IN THE POLICE HELICOPTERS WHICH WORK THE AREA COVERED BY HIS FORCE . HE AND CAROLINE CELEBRATED THEIR SILVER WEDDING ANNIVERSARY IN 2001. HE IS DUE TO RETIRE IN 2007 AT AGE 50. THE BOYS ARE ALL GROWN UP AND WORKING. NONE OF THEM HAVE FOLLOWED IN THEIR FATHER'S FOOTSTEPS.

THE END

EXPLANATION OF TERMINOLOGY

Aft - Toward the rear or stern of a ship or boat

Bagging Off - Sexual Intercourse, see also Egyptian gymnastics & Counterpane Hurdling.

Ballast - Any material used to weight a ship down in the water to increase stability or weight. In a submarine this is water, which is flooded in and blown or pumped out. As the crew eats food, drink fresh water or use any consumable material, seawater has to be flooded into the boat to compensate for the change in weight or the boat will rise to the surface.

Boiler Room - Area in a ship where water is heated to provide steam to turn engine turbines.

Bilge - Area at the bottom of a ship where water leaks and condensation gather to be pumped overboard.

Bomber - Ballistic missile submarine.

Bomber Queen - A crew member serving on a ballistic missile submarine.

Bomb Lift - Used to carry bombs and ammunition from the magazine to the flight deck in an aircraft carrier.

Bulkhead - The walls or vertical partitions in a ship. These could be either watertight or non-watertight.

Cap Tally - Band around a sailor's cap upon which the name of the ship to which he belongs is embroidered in gold.

Casing - Narrow upper deck of a submarine

Casing sentry - Rating responsibility for security on submarine while alongside. See also Trot Sentry

Catapult - Steam operated device for launching aircraft from the deck of aircraft carries. No longer used since the use of the Harrier Jump Jet was introduced.

Chimney Corner - An area on a submarine designated for the crew to smoke

Club swinger - Member of the Naval Physical Training branch, so called because of the crossed Indian clubs, which make up the branch badge on their uniform.

Commission - Either a promotion to officer or the period of time in which a ship or submarine is part of the active fleet of the Royal Navy. Submarines never go out of commission whereas surface ships are decommissioned to go to refit for extended period.

Control Room - Area, generally toward the centre of the submarine from which it is commanded and controlled.

Counterpane Hurdling - The act of sexual intercourse. See also Bagging Off & Egyptian Gymnastics

Court Martial - A military court.

Coxswain - Senior Naval Seaman rating in a submarine responsible for discipline and, in smaller submarines, victualling (food) and medical care of the crew.

Daily Orders - Document detailing duty personnel and ship's daily routine.

Defaulters - A court like proceedings overseen by a senior officer to punish those who have contravened The Queens Regulations for the Royal Navy

Divisional Officer - An officer in charge of a division, a section of the ship's company or crew.

Draft - A posting to another ship or establishment.

Draft Chit - Order for a naval rating to move from one ship or establishment to another.

Drafting Preference Card - A card available for completion by ratings in which they are able to state a preference for which base and ship they want to serve in. Administered by the Naval Drafting Office who decide on postings for all naval ratings.

Draught - Depth of a ship's hull beneath the surface. Normally read from markings painted on the hull.

Earth - Leakage of electricity from a circuit to the ships superstructure causing a circuit breakdown.

Egyptian Gymnastics - The act of sexual intercourse. See also Bagging Off and counterpane hurdling.

Familygram - A thirty-word message sent by the wife to the submarine each week, transmitted by radio from the home base. No reply is possible and this is the only contact a crewmember has with his family whilst at sea. Also known as a grumblygram.

Faslane - Submarine Base in Helensburgh, Scotland, situated on the Gareloch.

First Lieutenant - Second in Command of a submarine. See also Jimmy

Forends - Torpedo compartment, also known as Weapons Stowage Compartment.

Forenoon - The period between 8am and midday

Funnel - Steel tubing passing the waste gases from the engines, through the ships structure to a point above the ship where the gases are ejected into the atmosphere.

Galley - Ship's kitchen

Gangway - A metal or wooden ramp used to board ships.

Gash - Rubbish.

Gib - Shortened name for Gibraltar

Grumblygram - See Familygram

Grunter - Naval Officer (see also Rupert)

Heads - Naval term for toilets

HQ1 - Control centre from which all firefighting and damage control is coordinated during an emergency aboard naval ships.

Hydroplanes - Horizontal fins operated hydraulically used to control the fore and aft angle of the submarine and therefore control depth.

Jimmy - First Lieutenant, second in command of a submarine.

Joining Routine - Carried out when joining a new ship or establishment. It involves getting rubber stamps, on a card, from all the various departments within the ship who need to know of the ratings arrival.

Killick - Leading Hand in the Royal Navy (see appendix A, Naval rank structure)

Knot - Measure of speed at sea equal to one nautical mile per hour. (One nautical mile = 2000 yards)

Locker - Small storage space for personal effects.

Magazine - Ship's storage area for weapons and ammunition.

Main Vent - Hydraulically operated valve at the top of a ballast tank which, when opened allows air out thus allowing water into the bottom of the tank causing a submarine to dive.

Make and Mend - Afternoon off, so called from the days of sail when sailors used the time off to "make and mend" clothes.

Married Quarter - Housing supplied by the Royal Navy for married men for which a rent has to be paid

Master at Arms - Chief Petty Officer (See Naval rank structure, appendix A) of the Naval Regulating Branch (see Regulating Branch) always addressed as "Master".

Matelot (pronounced matterlow) - The French term for a sailor used by Royal Navy ratings to describe themselves.

Mess (deck) - Living space for naval ratings where sleeping and socializing is carried out. In smaller ships and submarines eating is also carried out in the mess.

MO - Medical Officer

NAAFI - Navy Army and Air Force Institute, an organization providing shops selling general goods in naval shore establishments and some larger ships.

Nutty - Any form of chocolate or confectionery.

Pay Off - Remove a ship or submarine from the active fleet, either to enter an extended refit or to be scrapped or sold.

Petty Officer - See appendix A—Rank structure

Plant the - The reactor onboard a nuclear submarine

Pontoon - Wooden (or other material) floating platform placed between the submarine hull and jetty to prevent damage to the hull.

Provost - Attachment of Naval Police who oversee discipline in a naval port or base area.

PT - Physical Training

Quartermaster - At sea the ship's helmsman responsible for steering the ship. In harbour the rating responsible for security at the head of the main gangway.

Rabbit - Souvenir

Rabbit Run - Trip for the purpose of purchasing souvenirs

Rating - Royal Naval other rank. See naval rank structure Appendix A

Regulating Branch Royal - Naval equivalent of the Royal Military Police

Request Form - Form completed to request leave, promotion or any other favour bestowed by the Royal Navy, including punishment

Requestman - Rating appearing before a Senior Officer for promotion, the award of any other advantage or to have any request considered.

Run Ashore - Visit to another port by a ship and its crew. Also a general term for a night out.

Rupert - A naval officer. (See also Grunter)

Salad Dodger - A person suffering from being a tad overweight.

Scablifter - Naval slang for a medical assistant

Sea Daddy - Experienced rating detailed to teach younger ratings the needs of the job.

Ship's Company - Collective name for the ship's crew.

Sick Bay - Naval Hospital or medical facility

Skimmer - Name given by submariners to any surface ship of the Royal Navy

Slops - Naval clothing stores. Naval Ratings are issued with their initial uniform and have to purchase replacements for those worn out or damaged. For this ratings receive a small kit upkeep allowance (KUA)

SSE Submerged Signal Ejector - used to fire smoke flares or grenade firing projectiles to the surface. Similar to a miniature vertically mounted torpedo tube fired by air or water

Stoker - Member of the naval Marine Engineering Branch

Subsistence - Cash paid to naval personnel who are required to live in hotels when at home or abroad.

Switchboard - Electrical panel controlling distribution of ship's electrical power

Tank the Submarine - escape Training Tower (SETT) at HMS Dolphin, Gosport

TI - Torpedo Instructor. Senior rating in charge of the torpedo compartment and weapons.

Tiff Artificer - A naval technician of either the electrical, mechanical or air electrical branch.

Torpedo Instructor - Senior rating in charge of the torpedo compartment and weapons.

Travel Warrant - Document issued to servicemen and women to pay for their travel. A servicemen is only granted a set number of travel warrants per year.

Trim System - A series of internal tanks around which water is pumped to keep the submarine evenly balanced or trimmed in the water.

Trot - Submarine berthing space

Trot Sentry - Rating responsible for security of submarine alongside a Trot. See also casing sentry.

Wardroom - Officer's mess, living accommodation for commissioned officers

Wankerchief - Cloth used to wipe the ejaculant during masturbation.

Watch - Period of duty. See appendix B, Watch System.

Wrecker - Artificer of the marine engineering branch who maintains the hull and domestic systems on a submarine. (The shipwright's branch which used to carry out this work was disbanded)

Wren - A member of the WRNS

WRNS - Women's Royal Naval Service

APPENDIX A
NAVAL RANK STRUCTURE

The Royal Naval rank structure is shown below. The equivalent ranks of the other two services are shown. My apologies to the Royal Marines whose rank structure is almost identical to the Army.

Royal Navy Ratings
Ordinary/Able Seaman
Leading Hand
Petty Officer
Chief Petty Officer
Warrant Officer

Royal Navy Officers
Midshipman
Sub Lieutenant
Lieutenant
Lieutenant Commander
Commander
Captain
Commodore
Rear Admiral
Vice Admiral
Admiral
Admiral of the Fleet

Army Other Ranks
Private
Corporal
Sergeant
Staff Sergeant
Warrant Officer 1

Army Officers
2nd Lieutenant
Lieutenant
Captain
Major
Lieutenant Colonel
Colonel
Brigadier
Major General
Lieutenant General
General
Field Marshall

Air Force Other Ranks
Leading Airman
Corporal
Sergeant
Flight sergeant
Warrant Officer

Air Force Officers
Pilot Officer
Flying Officer
Flight Lieutenant
Squadron Leader
Wing Commander
Group Captain
Air Commodore
Air Vice-Marshall
Air Marshall
Air Chief Marshall
Marshall of the RAF

APPENDIX B
NAVAL WATCH SYSTEM

The Royal Navy splits its day into seven periods called watches. In surface ships these are as shown below. However, in the submarine service the crew normally work in either two or three watch systems, i.e., either six hours on six hours off or four hours on eight hours off.

MIDDLE WATCH	Midnight to four am.
MORNING WATCH	Four am to eight am
FORENOON WATCH	Eight am to midday
AFTERNOON WATCH	Midday to four pm
FIRST DOG WATCH	Four pm to six pm
SECOND DOG WATCH	Six pm to eight pm
FIRST WATCH	Eight pm to midnight.

Printed in the United Kingdom
by Lightning Source UK Ltd.
116158UKS00001B/259-261